Literacy-Based Speech and Language Therapy Activities

Successfully Use Storybooks to Reduce Planning Time, Easily Work in Groups, and Target Multiple Communication and Academic Goals

Scott Prath & Phuong Palafox

Bilinguistics, Inc.

Published by Bilinguistics, Inc.

For more information, contact Bilinguistics, Inc. or visit us at: www.bilinguistics.com.

The terms storybook intervention, literature-based intervention and shared story reading are used interchangeably in this book.

ISBN-13: 978-0692886199 (Bilinguistics Speech & Language Services)

ISBN-10: 0692886192

This book is dedicated to Maritza Jacobs, our office manager, who has kept the Bilinguistics world spinning through the publication of 7 books, 40 online courses, and an unquantifiable number of speech therapy sessions and evaluations.

Introduction

We have been studying literacy-based intervention for the better part of a decade, have given numerous presentations, written papers, and have created a plethora of activities to use with our favorite stories. Most importantly, we have spoken with YOU to gain ideas, insight, and inspiration. We have heard the requests for these materials to be readily available to speech-language pathologists and educators across the country. And more than just templates, you wanted to know HOW we use these materials to help our students improve. The development of this literacy-based therapy book stemmed from teamwork, collaboration, feedback, and commitments to create effective therapy materials that can be easily implemented and utilized (especially with the busiest of workloads and schedules).

Why narratives and storybooks?

As educators, we rely heavily on narrative abilities when assessing our students' skills. We ask children to tell us about events, retell stories, write about events in their journals, and answer questions about stories or passages they read. We then analyze and judge the grammar and content of their story, the order of events, the semantic complexity, and the narrative elements. Finally, employing the full power of our professional wisdom, we determine whether a child is "within normal limits" or not. Heavy stuff if you think about it. Those of us who signed up for this profession are proud to take this challenge head on and make decisions calmly and seriously. But what do we do at this point? WHAT DO WE DO!? This is where this book comes in.

Storybooks provide a platform to address academic needs and therapeutic goals simultaneously while accounting for social and cultural factors.

We are here to tell you that a child's linguistic abilities can be stretched, grown, strengthened, built – brought up to what the world deems "within normal limits" and surpassed. Not in years but in months. And YES!, even when their culture is different, when they speak another language, and when their situation dictates that no one at home reads or has any familiarity with academic expectations. One other thing…are you sitting down? This not only works better than many of the other interventions, but it is really fun, too. High levels of learning coincide with high levels of engagement. That means for both your students and YOU! The use of storybooks and the activities suggested here have the power to reengage us in our profession while the students are having fun and tearing through their goals.

But I already use storybooks with my students. How is this different?

You are an educational professional who has probably used fiction and non-fiction books throughout your career. In writing this book we tackled research in speech-language pathology, education, and library science (see part 1) to assure that every minute of contact has a tremendous impact. Some research findings really caught us by surprise but when we created intervention based on that research, we saw huge growth.

Here are some examples:

You, like most educators, probably tell a story or read a book better than every grandmother on the planet. But have you ever thought about how you organize pre- and post- reading activities? What if I told you that I have used a single book for three weeks of speech therapy and didn't even open the book until the second week? What if I told you that I have a post-reading game-making routine that the kids enjoy so much that they want to skip recess for it? More on this in Section 3.

If you serve children from diverse cultures, did you know that there are five narrative elements that are shared by most cultures and another seven that differ between cultures? Focus on the five shared elements first and watch a child's story evolve. More on this in Section 2.

Yes, if you are reading this, you love books as much as we do. But did you know that the library science folks classify children's books into eight types? These eight narrative types give you the power to turn on movies in the child's brain so they can more easily replay (retell) the story with exquisite detail. Check out Section 6 to learn about these eight predictable narrative types and how to successfully create games.

Do you want to know what is truly unique about this book? It was written by people who:

1) have caseloads
2) are published researchers
3) serve bilingual children, and
4) work in low socio-economic neighborhoods.

Basically, this book was written by people who are very similar to you. We demand evidence to back things up. We work with large, diverse

YOU CAN NEVER TEACH SOMEONE SOMETHING THAT THEY DO NOT KNOW. YOU CAN ONLY BRING WHAT THEY DO KNOW TO A HIGHER LEVEL OF AWARENESS.

GALILEO GALILEI

caseloads. We need to address multiple goals simultaneously while working with groups of children. This is why we have become huge proponents of literacy-based intervention. It holds up against the reality of our jobs and contributes to academic and communicative growth at the same time. All you need to do is keep using storybooks while you hone in on six key areas to make your already great intervention more impactful.

How is this book organized?

This book is organized into 6 sections that will give you the all the buy-in, background, activity ideas, and materials you need to produce powerful literacy-based intervention.

1. The Research Behind Why Literacy-Based Intervention Works

You are smart and probably have a lot of letters behind your name and years of experience to prove it. You need facts and proof before you buy in to a new philosophy. We are researchers as well as practitioners and know that there is a huge gap between what goes on in academic research and what gets tested out in the schools and clinics. It is no one's fault. It is hard to do research when you have a caseload. And at the university, it is hard to find professionals and campuses to participate in a study. While this is true, it is not an excuse. In the first section, we highlight some important research to show why literacy-based intervention is a good use of our time.

2. Improving Story Narratives of Children from Diverse Cultures

How do we decide if narrative difficulties are due to an impairment, second-language influence, or cultural difference? This section highlights how culture and language shape the way children recount events and tell stories. By understanding differences in narrative styles, we can more successfully assess why a child is not producing or recalling stories as we would expect. Here is how it works:

- Five narrative elements are shared by most cultures (initiating event, attempt, consequence, resolution, and setting)
- Seven narrative elements are typically different (internal response, discourse markers, embedded stories, causal relations, causal chain, and protagonist identification)
- We would expect the first five to be present regardless of culture or language. If they are not in a child's story, we target them in intervention.
- We respect the cultural difference of the other seven and can teach (or share with teachers) what would be expected in a Western classroom.

3. How to Use Storybooks in Speech-Language Intervention

There is no shortage of books and printables for speech therapy. Research any storybook online and the internet will serve up an infinite number of cute and probably applicable activities. We present nationally on literacy-based intervention and the questions always boil to: "How do I do this well?" That is what this section is about.

After reading this section, you will be able to take any activity including *your* favorite storybook and design therapy that lasts for several weeks. We provide pre-, during-, and post-reading explanations and activities to assist in making your literacy-based intervention applicable to all age groups and disorder classes. We discuss scaffolding techniques to continually raise the bar on your students' progress, introduce brain-based strategies to keep them highly motivated and engaged, and tackle how to involve teachers and parents in the progress you are making.

4. Assessing What to Work on, Choosing Goals, and Taking Data

This section gives us the tools to know exactly what to work on and the means to strategically tie our therapy to communication goals and requirements of the curriculum. We will walk step-by-step through a child's story to see what is present and what is missing. We show how to write concrete, measurable goals and introduce you to an online goal bank where the work has already been done for you in Spanish and English. We then provide specific curriculum-aligned objectives (e.g. Common Core, TEKS in Texas) related to literacy-based intervention and tips for how to collect data along the way!

5. Literacy-Based Intervention Templates

We provide dozens of templates with examples of how they can be implemented in your therapy today. All activities found in this book are designed to be:

- Easily reproducible
- Used individually or in groups
- Applicable to almost any book
- Used on a variety of goals simultaneously
- Built around communication objectives and aligned to the curriculum

6. Creating Incredible Games that Match Story Content

Have you ever heard this?

"Speech therapists just play games."

Rather than defend ourselves, why don't we completely own it? In Section 6 we introduce you to a way to classify narratives into eight categories of "Predictable Books." This classification system is used to describe the narrative structure of a book. By understanding the direction that a story flows, we can create board games that rapidly boost the linguistic output of our students and clients.

As a quick example, *Where the Wild Things Are* is a "Circular Story." Max leaves his bedroom, crosses the ocean to where the Wild Things are, sails back across the ocean, and returns to his bedroom. Students who built this board game told an extremely complex and detailed story. More importantly, they understood this type of predictable story deeply.

Building gaming into our therapy enables something that we love to experience: Students are highly engaged and at the same time are generating incredibly rich expressive language.

Appendices: Great Books for Literacy-Based Intervention

We have all used storybooks with children that have completely bombed. Conversely, we have all seen children glued to stories that are bizarre at best. What is going on? We end with a list of great books for speech and language intervention that are organized by grade and topic.

So please, step into our world. In this world, the things that the children enjoy the most *are* the things that also get great results. In this world, we laugh and enjoy our jobs as much as the children do. In this safe place, we learn the entire time we are teaching. We learn about our children, about cultures, about foreign places, and are reminded of why we became educators in the first place.

Please join us,

Scott Prath & the Team at Bilinguistics

Contents

1. The Research Behind Why Literacy-Based Intervention Works

Through studies on race, culture, gender, socio-economic status, and educational experience, we are increasingly able to understand differences that govern the students that we serve. Our job as educators, is to identify whether a student is performing academically at an expected grade level. When this is not the case, we identify how we can intervene to bring performance up to grade level. Much of how we diagnose and intervene is based on our appraisal of the narrative that a student generates.

Storybooks have long been used as educational tools. They provide a structure for teaching concepts while keeping the student engaged and interested. Story structure additionally assists in retention and retrieval of classroom concepts due to familiarity with stories, repetition, and formulaic patterns. Book themes can be selected to allow students to explore fantasies, learn more about the real world, further students' knowledge about current classroom subjects, and introduce new topics. The benefits of literacy-based lessons have led to an increased use of storybooks in intervention.

Storybooks are beneficial to the work of speech-language pathologists (SLPs) from both an educational and a practical perspective.

1) The use of storybooks provides an excellent way to keep students engaged while addressing their speech and language goals.

2) Storybooks can be used with all ages and cultures to address a wide range of goals, including articulation, semantics, syntax, comprehension, pragmatics, and discourse skills.

3) Clinicians can work at different levels depending on each student's needs ranging from decontextualized discrete skills to skills that require more global processing, such as inferring meaning in stories, understanding characters' feelings, and producing story sequence.

4) Clinicians can use story themes and contexts to help students generalize skills learned in storybook reading to other settings.

5) On the practical side, using sets of storybooks with activities increases the efficiency of the often busy SLP by decreasing preparation time once the materials have initially been created.

6) Parents can easily become a part of the treatment process at home, which can greatly increase learning and retention of new skills.

7) Our role as SLPs is to align to the general education curriculum and using storybooks in intervention enables us to do this with ease.

The Benefits of Shared Reading

Researchers consistently have found that students with language learning difficulties have benefited from literacy-based intervention techniques. Shared reading activities have been shown to aid in students' overall development, including social-emotional, language, and academic development. By providing a model or visual experience, books can promote social-emotional development by helping students identify with and understand complex emotions, such as guilt, pride, and shame (Doyle and Bramwell, 2006).

Shared reading activities can also help students learn the language necessary to talk about their emotions. Such socio-emotional development has been shown to contribute to students' academic success (Denham, 1998; Zins, 2001). Storybooks promote language development by providing concurrent exposure to oral and written language (Teale and Sulzby, 1986). As Westby (1991) noted, narratives provide a bridge that connects oral communication to social interaction and writing. This allows students to learn new information and promotes development in different areas that contribute to academic success.

While books have been used as part of therapy for many years, current studies have found numerous benefits from the use of broader literacy-based intervention techniques.

- Shared reading experiences have been found to have a positive effect on students' overall oral language skills (DeBaryshe, 1993), as well as more specific skills.
- Storybook reading has been found effective for improving social language, such as establishing and maintaining joint attention and promoting conversational turn taking (Bruner, 1978).
- Literacy-based intervention also has been used successfully for vocabulary and grammar development by increasing vocabulary and by increasing the understanding of word relationships and complex sentence structures (Crowe, Norris, and Hoffman, 2000).
- Shared reading experiences give adults an opportunity to provide students with examples of language structures and vocabulary that they are not yet able to employ independently (Beed, Hawkins, and Roller, 1991; Bruner, 1978).

In addition to promoting growth in oral language development, shared reading experiences also provide an important link to literacy development. Reading to students promotes a greater eagerness to read, exposes students to printed materials they are not yet able to read independently, and provides them with positive reading role models. Reading also promotes a greater eagerness to read. This is important because students are already learning-to-read in Pre-K. By 4th grade they are reading-to-learn. Shared-reading contributes greatly to this shift.

Where Speech Therapy and Literacy Meet

In our jobs, it is the expectation that our work enables academic growth. That is what special education is for right?

We spend a lot of time looking for ways beyond our therapy to further support our students. When it comes to literacy, I would like to make the case that speech therapy and literacy goals already overlap and we are already doing a good job at supporting both. However, we probably aren't doing a good job letting people know just how well we are supporting them.

Take a look at this chart. Any of these words look familiar to you? Many speech therapy and literacy goals are often one-and-the-same.

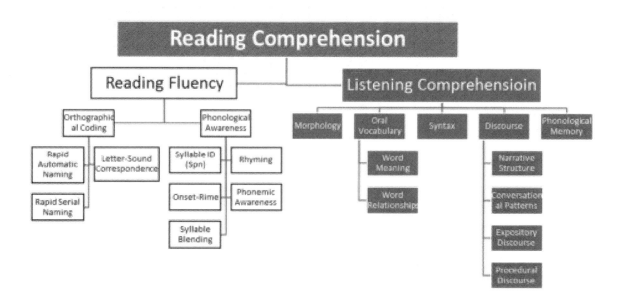

According to current research, children with speech and language difficulties often present with co-occurring reading difficulties, so speech-language pathologists working in all settings, can support students' reading acquisition and comprehension through their intervention. Additionally, children with language delays often need more frequent instruction that is shorter in duration. The size and repetitive nature of books allows us to accommodate different levels of language processing.

Flex your Language Expertise

Understanding the symbiotic relationship between reading difficulties and communication development helps practitioners design and implement appropriate intervention programs for monolingual and bilingual children. Many students who exhibit communication disorders often have difficulties acquiring reading skills. By understanding language development and reading skills acquisition, therapy can be targeted to meet underlying oral language needs in conjunction with reading fluency and comprehension skills. Such an approach enables SLPs to apply language expertise to struggles in reading.

One of the key goals in elementary education is teaching children to read. Acquiring reading skills is based on two basic areas: decoding and comprehension.

Decoding

In early elementary school, instruction focuses on learning phonemes, rhyming and decoding simple words to apply meaning. As children reach the later elementary school years, students have developed reading fluency, the ability to decode with fluidity, and are building their syntax, semantics, and discourse skills. Reading acquisition requires the integration of many skills, including but not limited to, sound-symbol awareness, automaticity in word recognition, vocabulary skills, and understanding of morphological and syntactic structures. Reading skills also transfer to writing skills in which children apply their knowledge of sounds to write words and practice their knowledge of morphology and syntax to formulate sentences to describe, define, and analyze. A variety of resources show that children's elementary reading abilities are used as predictors for future reading abilities, high school dropout rates, and effective communication abilities (Lipka and Siegel, 2007; Morais, Mousty, Kolinsky, Hulme and Joshi, 1998).

Reading Comprehension

Reading success is related to reading comprehension. Some language models show that while reading fluency and decoding skills are a component of reading comprehension, children also need to gain knowledge of morphology, oral vocabulary, syntax, phonological memory, and aspects of discourse (Teal and Sulzby, 1986). Children need to be able to understand narrative structures, actively access vocabulary, and interpret

incoming information from spoken and written sources (Lesaux and Siegel, 2003). SLPs help build a stronger foundation for these reading skills by targeting pre-literacy skills and spoken language. We also have a hand in helping our students acquire a written system by addressing letter-sound correspondence, rhyming, and sound blending.

Easily show how your speech therapy and reading goals are connected

Our speech therapy is drenched with reading comprehension and decoding support. We just need the right information to validate what we are already doing.

Here is what the American Speech-Language-Hearing Association (ASHA) has to say about speech therapy and reading: SLPs play a critical and direct role in literacy development, due to established connections between spoken and written language.

- Spoken language is the foundation for reading and writing
- Spoken language and reading and writing build on each other
- Children with speech-language impairment often have difficulty reading
- Instruction in spoken language can affect growth in reading and writing

This is a clear directive from our governing body: Treat communication and literacy simultaneously. The following five areas of research should give you all the buy-in that you need to know that literacy-based intervention has far reaching benefits and positive implications.

1. Statistics on Reading Deficits and Language Impairments

- 52% of children with language impairment also have reading difficulties (Tomblin, Zhang, Buckwalter and Catts, 2000)

- Poor reading skills have an ongoing, negative influence on vocabulary and language development (Catts and Kamhi, 2005)
- Reading comprehension skills in third grade were the best predictors of high school dropouts (California Dept. of Education, 2007)
- Children with language delays are likely to need more frequent instruction that is shorter in duration (Van Daal, J., et al 2007)
- Language of instruction should be kept at a suitable level of complexity and clarification to better accommodate children's speed of oral language processing (Rice, Bishop, and Leonard, 2000)

2. Socio-Economic Status (SES) as a factor

- Children from higher SES homes (due to social, language, and literacy enhancement abilities) are advanced in later reading achievement (Raz and Bryant, 1990)
- Children from higher SES homes are more successful in making the transition from "learning to read" to "reading to learn" (Campbell, Kelly, and Mullis, 2001)

3. Research looking at Reading Fluency

- There is a strong relationship between early language and phonological awareness/sensitivity and later reading and spelling development (Treiman, Hulme, and Joshi, 1998)
- Phonological Awareness:
  o Is a strong predictor of reading fluency, especially in orthographically inconsistent systems, in which one letter-sound combination can make more than one sound depending on the context.
  o Is more taxed in orthographically inconsistent systems (e.g. English) than in orthographically consistent systems (e.g. Spanish, Greek)
  o Phonological awareness and letter naming in Kindergarten predicted at-risk or typical reading development in Grade 3 for ESL and monolingual students

4. Efficacy of Intervention

- Engaging children in reciprocal verbal interactions that support the child in producing more linguistically complex dialogues directly facilitates the development of children's language proficiency and indirectly supports the development of their reading skills
- Both visual and verbal models of intervention resulted in gains in reading comprehension for adequate decoders/poor "comprehenders" (Carmichael, Callingham, Watson, and Hay, 2009)

5. Research Looking at Reading Comprehension

- Early language development is a precursor and good predictor of children's early reading development (Teal and Sulzby, 1986)
- Improving vocabulary and word knowledge is an important part of developing reading comprehension (Linan-Thompson, Vaughn, Prater, and Cirino, 2006)
- Processing resources, such as working memory, may more strongly influence word learning and reading ability than the availability or knowledge of language structures (Gilliver and Byrne, 2009)
- Semantic skills at age 3 and phonological awareness at age 6 both predicted reading skills at age 16 (Frost, Mencl, Sandak, Moore, Rueckl, Katz, and Pugh, 2005)

2. Improving Story Narratives of Children from Diverse Backgrounds

The narrative styles of children from English-speaking and non-English-speaking homes vary from culture to culture. That is to say, how a child tells a story, includes details, and conveys meaning is influenced by language, social class, and beliefs (Shiro, 1998). As educators, we rely heavily on narrative abilities when assessing our students' skills. We ask children to tell us about events, retell stories, write about events in their journals, and answer questions about stories. We then analyze and judge the grammar and content of their story, the order of events, the semantic complexity, and the narrative elements. Consider, however, that a child's stories are different than we expect because his culture and life experiences have taught him a different script. How do we decide if missing elements are due to an impairment or cultural difference? For example, what if a non-mainstream culture dictates that a story be ordered differently than in mainstream culture, or perhaps another culture places great importance on a story attribute that is not significant in mainstream American culture?

Further, the complexity of a child's story is considered in the diagnosis of language impairment, as well as in the selection of intervention goals. Common deficits include difficulty sequencing story events, difficulty identifying the main idea, problem and solution, and difficulty answering "WH" questions about a story. How should we use evaluation materials if they have not taken this child's culture into account?

Let's begin with research behind differences in narrative abilities and conclude with examples of how to:

1) easily determine what your student's current narrative includes
2) intervene successfully in the classroom and in language therapy

Narrative Elements that are Common to Most Cultures

The aspects of discourse and manner of oration that a speaker employs to tell his or her story vary from culture to culture. Initiating events, attempts, consequences, and resolutions are episodic features that are common to stories in most cultures. Contrarily, the uses of an internal response, discourse markers, listener roles and participant roles, are all culturally specific. Below are two quick reference charts with narrative elements that may be different across cultures and elements that most cultures share.

Narrative Elements that are **<u>Culturally Specific</u>**

Narrative Element	Definition	Example (3 Little Pigs)
Internal Response	An emotional response to the initiating event	The pigs were scared at the prospect of having to leave home.
Discourse Markers	A word or phrase that does not change the meaning of the sentence.	"well," "now," "then," "you know"
Embedded stories	Flashbacks and other cues that may impact the listener's experience.	The pigs had built their houses based on something that had happened to their father.
Causal Relations	The relationship between an event (the *cause*) and a second event (the effect).	The wolf blew the straw house down *so* the pig ran as fast as he could to his brother's house.
Causal Chain	A series of causal events that lead from beginning to end.	Story progresses from the straw house, then the stick house, and finally the brick house.
Protagonist Identification	Identification of the main protagonist in the story within the first scene.	Once upon a time there were three little pigs…

Narrative Elements that are **Common to Most Cultures**

Narrative Element	Definition	Example (3 Little Pigs)
Initiating Event	The incident which introduces the central conflict in a story.	Mom said it was time to live on their own.
Attempt	The protagonist's attempt to solve the problem.	The 3 pigs attempted to build houses.
Consequence	The results of the attempt (i.e. whether or not the goal was attained).	The houses were built.
Resolution	Whether or not the super-ordinate problem was resolved.	A house's strength/value was proportionate to the effort put into building it
Setting	The physical or temporal context of the story.	The country.

Which narrative elements are universal?

The presence of certain narrative elements and their use are culture specific. Organization, content, and meaning create a narrative structure that is part of every language. However, this universal nature only goes so far as to explain the broader components of a narrative. The way a child organizes his stories, the content he includes, and the meaning projected all vary as a result of cultural and linguistic influence.

Narrative development has been shown to be highly significant in the acquisition of complex language and literacy skills. Comprehension of large tasks, sequencing, interpretation of time-ordered events, and expository skills all require some skill that has been developed along with narrative abilities. Studies that have primarily focused on English-speaking monolinguals suggest that narrative development can reveal basic elements of academic readiness (Gutierrez-Clellen 2002).

How does narrative development change as a child gets older?

A natural increase in complexity is evident in different aspects of a story's composition as a child gets older. Clausal compliments expand from simple (They came.) to complex (We thought that they were coming.). Stories transition from being egocentric (I liked it) to awareness of other characters' thoughts (He was angry). Understanding of time is even relative to narrative development as a child moves from present-tense stories to working in the past. The majority of the research that we have available to us provides an explanation of narrative development in English. If narratives develop differently among different cultural and language groups, then criteria that have been developed for English may not be accurate for evaluating the non-mainstream population.

How can differences in narrative ability affect academic performance?

Spanish-speaking children continue to perform more poorly than other children on national indicators of achievement. The disparity between success rates of cultural groups may be the result of the testing criteria and not indicative of the Spanish-speaking population's intelligence or ability. The tests include identifying facts from written passages, making inferences from passages, searching for specific information from a passage, and meshing ideas (Gutierrez-Clellen, 2002). It is expected that a child use the text and his or her own world knowledge in order to answer the questions. When a child's personal knowledge differs from that of mainstream America, it can only be expected that a discourse, story recount, or story telling will not match the standards currently used in assessing narrative ability. As a result, that student's narrative abilities might be underestimated.

How can a story narrative be useful for intervention?

Children use story telling as a way to interact and share information about what is going on in their daily lives. These stories are a quick snapshot of overall linguistic ability. The understanding of what goes into a story and the ability to tell a story require phonological, morphological, syntactic, semantic, and pragmatic knowledge. Additionally, having a child tell a story provides the clinician with an uninterrupted flow of discourse from a child, thereby avoiding certain artificialities of data from conventional elicitation (Klecan-Aker and Colson, 2009).

CULTURE & SECOND LANGUAGE

Is how we ask children to tell a story different than how their parents ask?

In a study on cultural variations in the construction of personal narratives, Melzi (2000) examined narrative elicitation styles of Spanish-speaking Central American mothers and English-speaking mothers with European origin. The results showed that the two groups differed in how they elicited a story, as well as what aspects of the narrative they chose to emphasize. European American mothers primarily focused on the organizational aspects of the narrative. The Central American mothers emphasized the conversational aspects of the narrative. The Spanish-speaking children had greater responsibility in recalling the story as their mothers played a listening role in the conversation. This is in contrast to the English-speaking children who acted as co-narrators with their parents. Melzi (2000) concluded that the elicitation styles correspond to the socialization goals of each culture. This suggests that conversational patterns are inherently different based on cultural demands.

Benefits of reading to children in their native language

We often hear this question from parents:

"Am I confusing my child by speaking and reading to him in

my native language?"

The answer? A resounding NO!!! Unfortunately, this idea is still propagated by well-meaning doctors and educational professionals. It makes sense on some level, right? The theory is that if a child is having difficulty communicating, then two languages would make matters worse. The truth is that the number of languages a child speaks does not contribute to communication deficits. What is important is the complexity of the language that is being used. If we are asking parents to interact in a language that is undeveloped and foreign to them, the child's communication will not grow sufficiently. If they provide a great language model, the linguistic abilities will transfer from one language to the other.

In great study about how beneficial it is for parents to read to their kids in their native language, Huennekens and Xu (2010) studied the impact of cross-linguistic storybook intervention on English language development in preschoolers. Researchers selected books that were available in the children's home language (Spanish, in this case) and in English. Parents were asked to read the books in their native language. Meanwhile, during school hours, teachers read the same books in English. During the period of time that parents and teachers were reading the same books, these preschoolers increased the frequency of their utterances, increased the length of their utterances, and increased their use of spontaneous interactions in the classroom. So, to sum it up—when parents read to their children in Spanish, the children's language skills in the English-speaking environment increased in frequency and complexity also. So…tell your parents to keep reading in their native language!

We are talking about the benefits of using books for speech, receptive language, expressive language and social-pragmatic gains. An important fact that we must talk about is the cultural gains a child and family receive from relishing in the literacy experience in their native language. When we are able to provide resources in a family's native language, we are honoring their language background, their experiences and their invaluable contributions to our country. These sentiments say, "Your native language is just as valuable as mine." Imagine receiving a book to read to your child in your most comfortable language versus a book that contains words that you may not understand and know how to read. We understand that this is not always possible and available; however, when books are sent home in a child's native language, the benefits are paramount.

How does socio-economic status (SES) affect narratives?

We address this complex topic with great caution. It is easy to stereotype, and the truth is that not everyone living in poverty is affected equally. As service providers, it is important to understand potentially harmful effects so we can identify when poverty is influencing our evaluation results and progress in intervention.

First, let's talk about the facts. Federal guidelines classify a family of four as living in poverty if the family's annual income is less than $24,257 (Proctor, Semega, and Kollar, 2016). Who is most affected by poverty? The poorest are children of color under the age of six (Children's Defense Fund, 2016). As of 2015, this equates to more than 14.5 million. That's one in five children, and we serve those children as SLPs.

We know that development differs, at times, for those from low-income communities. There are differences in brain development between children from high-, middle-, and low-income families. Cognitive functions affected by poverty include working memory, impulse regulation, and language skills (Noble, Norman, and Farah, 2005). When coupled with chronic stressors, the ability to cope is also compromised. Now, let's think about the emotional development. Long-term poverty can impact emotional development. Jensen's Emotional Keyboard Model (Jensen, 2008) helps us understand which emotional skills (e.g., anger and surprise) are hardwired into all of us and which ones need to be explicitly taught. Oftentimes, we see school expectations requiring skills, such as cooperation and patience, that require direct teaching.

Poverty can also negatively impact language development, reading, and school performance. Children from limited-language environments hear the most commonly occurring words (Weizman and Snow, 2001). Their receptive vocabularies can be less than 5,000 words while other children understand 20,000 words (Montgomery and Evans, 2009). Children in poverty average 25 hours of reading at home as opposed to 1,000 hours of reading in language-rich homes (Whitehurst, Adamson, and Romski, 1997). This puts children from low SES backgrounds at an academic disadvantage.

Shiro (1998) illustrated this point in a study of Venezuelan school children in which she sought to identify whether or not appropriate use of evaluative talk differed across age, gender, and class. The use of listener feedback and critique (evaluative talk) is the basis for learning competent story telling. Evaluative feedback was studied in the creation of fictional and personal narratives. Shiro found that evaluative language varied considerably with age and social class. The stories expanded in correlation with an increase in age. Not only did stories improve with social status, but it was also noted that children of a lower social class had difficulty even producing fictional narratives (Shiro, 1998).

Fortunately, the brain is an elastic organ that continually responds to input. Strategies, such as creating a positive, high-achieving environment, impacts social and behavioral outcomes. Making connections by basing lessons on topics students actually know about can make a huge difference during therapy. We will also talk about brain-based strategies in the intervention portion of this book. We have an important role on our campuses and can use our communication knowledge to give a massive boost to children from all walks of life.

Narrative Elements that are Specific to Spanish and English

In his cross comparison of the traditional American "sharing time" with the Spanish equivalent "La Ronda," Poveda (2002) identified narrative elements that were both shared and culturally specific. Existence, organization, and content of each session were similar. That is to say that both cultures valued having the sharing time as part of their curriculum, structured the experience similarly, and covered similar topics. However, the goals of the sessions were different. Oral narratives of Spanish children had moral themes. These children used the event to demonstrate a sense of themselves in relation to their community. English narratives in turn were more individualistic and child-centered. Different narrative abilities were born out of similar situations. The difference could be derived from the value that each culture put on different story components, thereby increasing the frequency of those types of stories and exposure (Poveda, 2002). The following page is a quick reference chart showing narrative differences between Spanish and English.

A Comparison of Narrative Elements in Spanish and English

	Spanish	English
Goal of most narratives	Moral themes. Spanish-speaking children may use an event to demonstrate a sense of themselves in relation to their community.	Individualistic/child-centered themes. English narratives focus on what is happening internally and externally to the main character.
Reaction	A character's reaction to an event or element may be atypical.	A character's reaction to an event is predictable.
Story Elicitation	Conversational aspects of the narrative are emphasized. Spanish-speaking children have greater responsibility in recalling the story. Mothers play a listening role.	Mothers focus on the organizational aspects of the narrative and English-speaking children may act as co-narrators with parents.
Grammar – meaning	Spanish relies on the inflection of morphemes, including verb forms.	English relies on manipulation of word order.
Grammar – syntax	Spanish employs verb forms not often used in English to show conditionality or actions that continue from the past. Spanish also has a flexible word order	English has a strict word order.
Acting as a listener or a participant	Spanish-speaking cultures often have the role of speaker *or* listener and may not simultaneously engage.	English-speaking cultures may tell a story together, ask questions, or interject during a story.

CULTURE & SECOND LANGUAGE

How does the grammar of each language affect story telling?

Differences in narrative type extend past what is purely influenced by culture. Grammatical variations can also be dictated by rules or sentiments of a host language. A study of Spanish and English highlights a multitude of these differences. Morphologically, English conveys variations in meaning by manipulation of word order. To accomplish the same task, Spanish relies on the inflection of the morphemes. Syntactically, Spanish will employ verb forms not often used in English to show conditionality or actions that have continued from the past. Spanish also enjoys more flexibility in word order. With the large culmination of differences, Silliman and colleagues (2002) noted that the application of Spanish or English monolingual norms to a group of bilingual children would be inappropriate, whether for research, educational, or clinical purposes.

Should different criteria exist for evaluating narratives of English and Spanish speakers?

Current research suggests that enough cultural, morphological, and syntactic differences exist between English and Spanish that separate narrative criteria should be formed for each language. In the same way that standardized test scores are inconclusive when testing non-mainstream populations, the norms that have been developed to evaluate narrative discourse are culturally biased. Education on narrative differences and the development of new standards need to take place. Otherwise, as Heath (1982) suggests, "evaluators who are unfamiliar with narrative style may misinterpret or fail to value the stories of children from diverse backgrounds."

Elicitation of narratives is a popular tool used by speech language pathologists to gain information on language abilities. Criteria have been established that can differentiate between productions that are typical of normal or language delayed children. However, research indicates that children who learn English as a second language may demonstrate patterns that are equivalent to language impaired children. The high number of Spanish-speaking children in special education programs qualifies this. If educational and therapeutic practices wish to use narrative development as criteria for evaluating a child, then they have to take into account how the development occurs in each language (Silliman, Bahr, Brea, Hnath-Chisolm, and Mahecha, 2002).

Can formal tests with narrative components still be used?

Portions of formal tests that elicit narratives should be scored while keeping the child's first language in mind. The *Preschool Language Scales*, 4th and 5th editions, include a narrative task in the expressive language portion of the test. The administrator reads a story and requests a recount, tells a story from a picture and requests a recount, and requests a spontaneous story from a picture. In each situation, the examiner tallies narrative components that are indicative of narratives from mainstream children. Poor performance, as determined by the standardized assessment, could result from differences in cultural expectations and result in reduced scores. Examiners should consider cultural variation in storytelling when evaluating the order and organization of a story. In addition to providing merit for story components, the development of the characters and social/moral aspects of their actions should receive attention as well.

How does typical narrative development differ from narrative development in a child with language impairment?

Children with language and learning impairments produce narratives with fewer different words, fewer total words, more grammatical errors, less content, and poorer use of cohesive devices (Swanson, Fey, Mills and Hood, 2005). Children with a history of language difficulties, even those dismissed from special education services, continue to need support in creating narratives throughout their academic career (Fey Catts, Proctor-Williams, Tomblin, and Zhang, 2004). The importance of narrative development should not be understated. As Gillam and Pearson (2004) pointed out, poor narrative abilities can affect intellectual, social, and academic development.

After a review of the research, intellectually it is easy to accept that an increase in narrative abilities enriches the student's message, improves classroom productivity, and shows the student the difference between their habitual narrative and what is expected academically. By learning a bit about culture and second-language needs, we see that it is obvious that different narrative styles exist between cultures and that these differences should be accounted for in therapy and evaluation. The question is, can we alter our evaluations and intervention to account for differences in narrative ability? The answer is a resounding YES! Not only *account* for differences but employ our innate love and use of storytelling to help children produce incredible language so that we can dismiss them from special education services. In the next section, we will learn how to provide amazing literacy-based intervention.

3. How to Use Storybooks in Speech Language Intervention

We are great at speech therapy, but what if we could magically triple our therapy materials and activities for the same amount of effort? Or reduce our planning by a third? Using research on literacy-based intervention and culture, we have created a structure for use before, during, and after book-reading to maximize a story's magical effects, both for us and our students.

This section is divided into 4 parts

1. Planning for Literacy-based Intervention Sessions

This section covers tips and tricks to rapidly plan for individual and group sessions and capture our work so that each year gets easier and easier.

2. Pre-Reading Activities – Before you Open the Book

There are many activities that can be undertaken before the we even open a storybook to maximize our efforts with the student, ensure comprehension of the story we are about to read, and increase the retention of all the new vocabulary that each book introduces. If you typically read the book in your first session, this is going to be eye-opening and has the potential of cutting your planning time in half.

3. Book-Reading Activities

Here is the part we are all most familiar with and where we are happiest – reading the book. But did you know that there are three ways to dramatically enhance your therapy? We will cover scaffolding strategies, brain-based learning, and story-grammar development. SLPs have shared that these activities have become the most enjoyable aspects of their work day.

4. Post-Reading Activities – After the Book is Closed

Do you move on to a new topic or book after you have finished a story? After reading the story, children finally understand the plot, have the vocabulary to talk about it, and the motivation to show what they know. This creates the perfect environment to write similar stories, tell the story, and create games that follow the character's adventures. Pre-reading activities cut your therapy planning in half. Post-Reading Activities extend your lesson plans and reduce planning even further.

1. Planning for Literacy-based Intervention Sessions

Cumulative Speech Therapy Planning

Before we even begin to start talking about planning, we need to have a conversation that we wish that someone had with us on day one. Year after year, we gear up for the new school year or a new clinic caseload. And, it seems like our job should get easier, right? Math is not my forte; however, the following Equation-of-SLP-Ease should be applicable:

According to my algebra, for every year of SLP-service I put in, my effort should feel less.... difficult. However, based on the input of SLPs, this is far from the truth. This is because our daily endeavors are not *cumulative*. Each time you put efforts toward creating materials, you need to organize, label, and keep the materials forever. I promise that you will have another student or group that will benefit from the same materials in the future. Keep the materials in one of the following, awesome therapy-keepers:

Option #1: A filing cabinet or foldering system

Most speech pathologists have stacks of books full of reproducible activities. The problem is, they are not typically divided by theme. For example, last week I was putting together materials for a book called Growing Things. I couldn't remember if a really cool sunflower activity that I saw was in the articulation book under "S," in a book on outdoor activities, or none-of-the-above. I never found it. Keeping one extra copy of the materials that you use in a themed-folder will allow you to easily access it for years to come.

Option #2: A clear box labeled for each storybook or unit

Many storybooks require physical items or bulky materials used to garden, create puppet shows, etc. The younger your audience, the more engaged they will be with physical manipulatives. As an example, my first-year supervisor had a closet full of clear bins labeled for each book she used. When it was time to use her box for *The Very Hungry Caterpillar*, she just pulled her box off the shelf, and she had her materials for an entire month.

Option #3: A shared drive

SLPs in several districts near us share all of their materials with each other on a shared drive. This puts the efforts of dozens of professionals at your fingertips. If you already have a space like this, it just might need some organizing or you may need to build a section dedicated to storybooks and alphabetized by title.

Reduce Speech Therapy Planning Time

Planning for intervention can sometimes take longer than the sessions themselves. By dedicating yourself to literacy-based intervention, you will find that there is a whole arsenal of materials and resources already available in your schools to save you massive amounts of time and simultaneously support the other professionals you work with. Here are five tips to enable you to quickly produce high-impact therapy materials to support the storybook that you are using.

1. Get buy-in from teachers

Is this your car? If so, know that as speech pathologists, we don't have to do this anymore!

Every week, teachers have materials, pages, and storybooks from the library already set out and planned. Borrow from them to reduce speech therapy planning time and the children will flourish when they can practice their communication using the same familiar book or object back in the classroom.

How important is it to you that you choose what you work on in therapy? I am not talking about the specific goals but the content. Does it really matter if we are working on /s/ words out of a random book or /s/ words that are about animals or some other academic topic? Choose the book or story that the teacher is focusing on in her classroom.

If we contact teachers and focus on *their* curriculum topics, then the child has a way to:

- Practice what you teach him
- Show off or interact with peers
- Practice their words on homework with parents

If we choose the topic that the teacher is working on, then she or he feels that:

- Their work is important
- We understand what is going on in the classroom

The law (IDEA 2004) states that we need to give access to the general education curriculum. By using books that are already being used in the classroom we can both create great therapy and abide by the law of the land. Easily find out what teachers are working on:

- Have teachers email you at the beginning of the week. You can send an automated email each week and ask that they can just respond in the subject line. Shapes and colors, Abraham Lincoln, etc.

SLP Confession

"I FIGURE OUT WHAT THE GRADE-LEVEL TEAMS' PLANNING TIME IS AND I SIT AND LISTEN. WITHIN A FEW MINUTES I KNOW WHAT TOPICS THEY WILL BE COVERING AND WHAT BOOKS THEY WILL BE USING. VOILA! I HAVE MY BOOKS FOR SPEECH THERAPY!"

- Ask as you pick up your students or when you are in the teacher lounge.
- Ask them to include you on emails if they submit their lesson plans each week.

2. Get buy-in from parents

Our days are hectic enough and trying to reach out to all parents continually is unfeasible. Yet, no one has a greater interest in seeing children succeed than their parents. We can easily make a cookie-cutter "Hi Parents" letter for each topic we address. It looks like this:

Hi parents,

This week we read _____. Ask your child to talk about the story and/or practice the following words.

We make these sheets once for each storybook and have them to give out for all the upcoming years. The parents are going through their homework anyways. This way they stay informed and engaged.

3. Lean on your colleagues

Chances are you work with SLPs ranging in age from 24 to 60. Chances are you also have staffing or in-service days that are used to focus on development.

Use the staff-development days, times, and colleagues that you already have, and create a place, electronic or virtual, where everyone can add materials related to the most common storybooks that you are using. You may be pleasantly surprised by the amount of content that your friends have already collected from their favorite books. The tech-savvy staff members can set up online folders organized by title for experienced SLPs to place their oodles of resources in.

4. Organize your materials by *THEME* not by sound

As a speech therapist, I am sure that this chart makes sense to you. But what if you showed this to someone who was not an SLP? How are these words even related? Our brain does not organize things like speech therapists do. I am not suggesting you buy anything new, just reorganize all your terrific materials based on the book you are reading.

snout	snow	snack
spin	spoon	spot
spade	spout	spy
steam	stew	stop

Here is an example of a double win. It is a list of 1) language vocabulary sorted by 2) articulation sounds to be used with books about growing things.

5. Choose books that align with the curriculum

As a young speech pathologist, I was confronted with a caseload that was so large and staggeringly diverse that it nearly brought an immediate end to my early career. I worked across two campuses with 65 Spanish-speaking students and conducted evaluations on another five campuses. Twenty-six of my students were in a 3-year-old half day program and many of them had multiple disabilities. What is the best way to continue exposure to what we focused on in therapy when I wasn't with my students?

Curriculum-based intervention materials can simultaneously enrich language and teach academic concepts. Choose books or stories that go along with the academic theme. This way:

- We give students multiple opportunities to practice their concepts back in the classroom
- They have the vocabulary to talk about the homework they are showing their parents
- We make teachers happy because they feel supported

Speech Therapy Inclusion – Reaping the Benefits of Working in the Classroom

Less than 30% of speech pathologists do speech therapy in the classroom. Yet, classroom-based therapy gives us the opportunity to:

- Improve our relationships with teachers
- Have our therapy map directly over academic goals
- Reduce our therapy planning by using the content and materials that teachers are developing each week

But how can we successfully make the transition from independent group therapy to reaping the rewards of collaborating with speech therapy inclusion?

6 Models for Co-teaching in Speech Therapy Inclusion

Let's talk about the six models for co-teaching to show how speech and language intervention can overlap with academic needs.

One Teaches - One Observes

The One Teaches – One Observes model is the most commonly reported model used by SLPs. We do gain information on what is going on in the classroom, but we don't directly have an impact. Overall, it is a great opportunity to see the grade level content.

One Teaches - One Assists

The One Teaches – One Assists model is successful in one-on-one cases and is most prevalent with assistant teachers helping out in the classroom. We can see directly where the child is struggling and supply support to successfully complete lessons.

Parallel Teach

In Parallel Teach, we don't split the content but we split the class in half. This allows you to interact with the children who need more attention. This is also an opportunity to observe typically-developing children and get *wowed* by how well they use language.

Station Teaching

In Station Teaching, you DO split the content. The teacher and SLP both do different things and then rotate through the students.

Alternative Teaching

Alternative Teaching is what we see most often with special education assistants. The teacher is teaching the main group and you pull a small group aside that needs specific instruction.

Team Teaching

The ultimate of all of these co-teaching models is Team Teaching. The SLP and teacher go back and forth. Each adds something to the lesson as it is presented. This works great when the SLP is presenting a language rich book or lesson, and the teacher, who knows the students, can differentiate the expectations of each child's response and work.

Start at the level that is most comfortable for you, and move up the spectrum. Co-teaching and specifically team-teaching, give us the opportunity to influence writing, influence language and narrative development, pronunciation, and address the general education curriculum. The better we are able to understand the requirements being put upon our students, the better we can help them excel.

Planning for a Diverse Caseload

Pre-planning is essential if you are working with students with multiple disabilities. It is one thing to adapt a session for students who are not communicating verbally. But what about the students who can't see or hear? Or what about students with mobility restrictions? We want to think about the book and activities from their point of view and identify ways that they can participate. The modifications table on the following page provides suggestions for modifying intervention for students with a variety of physical and behavioral impairments as well as ways to modify for varying levels of communication.

Supporting Low-Incidence Populations

It is now time to talk about those of us who have the important job of supporting our low-incidence populations. Who does this refer to? This applies to students and clients we see with autism, intellectual disabilities, low vision and blindness, hard-of-hearing and deafness, significant developmental delays, physical impairments and complex health needs.

So, why is this applicable in a book related to literacy-based activities? First, let's talk about the academic expectations for students in general education. It relates to academic and literacy outcomes. In contrast, IEPs for our students in low-incidence populations are typically reflective of social skills and functional life skills. Know that it is possible to address the functional *and* academic literacy needs of students—with meaningful accommodations and modifications in place.

First, we want to point out that there are three ways to read: reading the book, looking at the pictures and acting out the story. With this idea in mind, think of how *all* students can read. We have seen a two-year old holding a picture book and talking about the pictures using one to two-word utterances (e.g., moo cow!) as the pages turn. This is reading. We have seen a group of high school students in a Life Skills classroom walk over to the classroom's library, choose a book, hold it correctly, turn the pages appropriately and view the visuals conveying the plots of the story. This is also reading. We have seen a fifth grader using a speech output device to tell a story using his Core Vocabulary—hang on. We have more on this at the end of this section!

Special Considerations for Low-Incidence Populations

Physical Impairments: For students with physical impairments, we must keep materials mobile so that they are easily accessible. Instead of requiring children to come up to the board, for example, we can use a small board that goes to the student.

Visual Impairments: For students with visual impairments we suggest using a variety of auditory clips or tactile objects that go with each lesson.

Auditory Impairments: For students with auditory impairments, supplement your instruction with a variety of visual aids and also suggest using specific signs to target concepts in the story.

Augmentative Communication: For students with AAC devices, create communication boards with the core vocabulary from the story. These can be low-tech images of the characters and places that the student can point at in order to answer questions.

Modifications Table

Here is an example of a modifications table that you can make for each story book you use. Fill out this table once and you will have it for all the years to come.

Impairment Considerations

Physical Impairments- Low Mobility	Felt board to reduce travel but increase participation. For example: animal cutouts on popsicle sticks, flashlight/light pointer
AAC devices	Visuals and Templates needed: Example: Go Talk 20, Switch Visuals, Topic vocabulary on Big Mac
Visual Impairment	Use objects from tactile schedule to symbolize curriculum vocabulary
Hearing impairment	Signs (mom, dad, school), AAC device, pictures/visuals, sentence strips
Behavior	Personal object/activity For example: characters on popsicle sticks

Communication Abilities

Nonverbal	Joint attention Use picture/word/sign to request preferred object/activity Identify curriculum vocabulary
Nonverbal + gestures	Follow directions Imitate CV, VCV, CVCV combinations (C = consonants, V = vowels)
Low verbal- 1 word	Produce CV, VCV, CVCV combinations Label objects and target specific vocabulary
Verbal	Expressive goals For example: Answer basic wh- questions, prepositions, and pronouns

Using Core Vocabulary to Support Literacy

When it comes to literacy and supporting our low-incidence populations, we need to talk about Core vocabulary. What is it? Core vocabulary words are high frequency, reusable, generic words. They comprise 80-90% of the words we use (e.g., want, more, put, I, mine, go, all done). Core vocabulary is important because it promotes generative language. In other words, your child is not limited to requesting nouns (e.g., I want cookie). And, by using Core vocabulary, you are giving your child access to 50-300 high frequency, re-usable words and variations of words. The best part is that he can use these words across a variety of events or activities throughout his entire life.

4 Tips for Using Core Vocabulary

Give Access: Please make sure you provide your child with a communication system. This could be the Core vocabulary board provided to you. This could also be a communication device you already own. Remember, give your child full access to a consistent communication system. This will give him the opportunity to let us know what he wants and how he feels, and let him give commentary on everyday activities. In our clinic and on our campuses, students have used the core vocabulary board to tell us they want (a request/want) to talk to a friend, they're mad (feelings) following a bowling spare and that something was funny (share in humor).

Model, Model, Model: If your student is still learning how to use a communication system, please model the language for him. Remember, we model language for babies for approximately 9-12 months before they utter their first "mama" or "dada." And, babies have likely heard the same word hundreds to thousands of times before saying it for the first time. So, we are going to model often. For example, you could point to "I," "want" and "go" every time you go somewhere.

Know Gail Van Tatenhove: Please refer to Gail Van Tatenhove's work for support in implementing a communication system. Her YouTube channel provides content and visuals for using these important communication systems: https://www.youtube.com/user/gvantatenhove.

Have fun: Know that communication, at the end of the day, is best used to create meaningful (and fun) experiences. I am also including the core vocabulary board I used for bowling. My students had a great time at bowling this year, and this created opportunities to talk about how they did, their feelings following each turn, and vocabulary for steps taken when bowling (e.g., putting on shoes, getting ball). So, have fun!

When it comes to literacy, use core vocabulary to give access to books. There are many educators and speech-language pathologists who have adapted books using core vocabulary. By searching "adapted books and core vocabulary," we found many resources on the internet. For example, Tar

Heel Reader (tarheelreader.org) is a collection of free, easy-to-use adapted books on a plethora of subjects. So, if your student is working on community helpers, you can type into their search engines and find 24 options! You can also make your own book and share it with fellow users of the site.

Finding the Best Books for Speech Therapy

Choosing the right book is crucial for engaging the students. The general criteria in choosing a book are that it must be age-appropriate, interesting to children, and have some pertinence to a student's speech or language goals. Books that are already in use in the classroom can have a dramatic effect on a student's success and level of confidence due to familiarity and repetition. Fortunately, the school environment abounds with resources and support to help in choosing books that meet your students' needs. We also created an Appendix at the end of this book with storybooks that are divided by grade and theme.

Librarians

Librarians are usually very helpful in choosing the appropriate level and themes for the students. They are very knowledgeable about book content and are insightful in suggesting books when a SLP describes what he or she hopes to accomplish with the book activity. Depending on the size of the school, librarians often know most of the students personally and can offer suggestions on popular topics with classrooms or specific students.

Classroom Teachers:

It is also a good idea to talk to the classroom teacher in order to get a schedule of themes that will be taught in the classroom. Repetition of topics gives a student confidence due to an already established knowledge base and familiar vocabulary. The repetition of themes also encourages carryover of speech and language goals into the classroom setting.

Internet Resources:

The internet is often the fastest and most used resource for finding books. By refining our search to specific articulation sounds or activities, we can find a ton of quick content online.

In Summary: How to make planning for speech therapy easy

We routinely have speech pathology graduate students working with us who need to know what to be planning for speech therapy before the kids arrive. What they might not have learned is that the first few weeks of therapy in the schools are pretty crazy. You have to get to know your students or clients, organize schedules, identify student needs, group them, and get them up and running. Here are four quick steps to rapidly plan therapy.

Find out what topic is being focused on each week

Aligning intervention themes with classroom topics increases exposure and use of vocabulary. It also provides a framework in which students can practice their new language skills. Identifying the current academic topic (e.g. oceans) dramatically reduces speech therapy planning because the teachers tend to have materials and books ready for us to copy from and use.

Go to the library and check out books on the topic

Using books to highlight a topic can empower students by giving them experience with the topic prior to practicing the skills that you are hoping for them to gain. Gather both fiction and non-fiction books about the theme/topic. Books provide vast numbers of pictures, references, and situations.

Copy an activity page for each student

Either search for the book topic materials on the internet or borrow something from the classroom teacher. Adapt the vocabulary or questions to the student's goals. Communication growth is stimulated by carryover into the classroom, reviewing of vocabulary, and shared participation by teacher and parents.

Cut/color/copy materials needed for each session

While planning for speech therapy, make sure your sessions are designed for fast assembly and distribution. Gather the materials needed and make the minimal preparations. Better yet, have your students gather and prepare their own materials and bolster their receptive communication by following directions!

SLP Confession

"I REVIEW GOALS AT THE START OF <u>EVERY</u> SESSION. MY KIDDOS KNOW EXACTLY WHY THEY COME TO SPEECH AND OVER TIME THEY CHEER ON THEIR PEERS BECAUSE THEY KNOW THEIR GOALS TOO!?

2. Pre-Reading Activities – Before You Open the Book

Before I began literacy-based intervention I would gather my students for therapy, do the greetings or explain the day, and pop open the book. Within the next 30 minutes I would probably do an activity and conclude the book. Good therapy, but it wasn't until I incorporated pre-reading activities that I began dismissing students at a startling rate.

When we work with diverse populations we can't make any assumptions about whether the child knows the stories, has books at home, has literate parents, speaks our language at home...

The list goes on and on. Remember that academic expectations are based on children from Western culture, who probably grew up being read to, who have an inherent knowledge of specific story structures, that were presented in their native tongue. This is absolutely fine, **we just can't make assumptions** that our students have this in place prior to entering our therapy room. This isn't just a cultural or second-language issue. Even children from Western cultures with impairments lack core linguistic abilities and benefit from creating a foundation to build their abilities. By creating pre-reading activities, we can rule out these possible influences so that we can concentrate strictly on the disordered areas.

Pre-reading activities engage the student prior to reading the story, introduce them to new vocabulary and historical events, and prepare them to comprehend the story in a more meaningful manner. Pre-reading activities are used to bridge gaps between a student's current skills and the targeted skills. Connecting to the child's background is essential. Without closing this gap, we are reading *at* the child, not to him (Coppola, 2004).

Great Pre-Reading Activities

Music

Music provides us with an engaging way to introduce new vocabulary for a topic. You can find a song on nearly any topic on the internet simply by searching: TOPIC + Song. We have created a list of songs related to some of the more common topics which you can see at www. bilinguistics.com/music-for-speech-therapy/. You can make your own play list or start grouping songs by topic to build your own library.

Let's use the Kindergarten topic BODY PARTS as an example. We could read Eric Carle's *From Head to Toe* and here are some songs that you could play:

English Song	Spanish Song
Head, shoulders, knees and toes	Cabeza, hombros, rodillas, pies
I am a Pizza	Soy una pizza
The Vowels	Las vocales
When Little Johnny Dances	Juanito cuando baila

We can choose a song and act out the body parts motions and even make supporting materials. Below are some activity example sheets for *When Little Johnny Dances*.

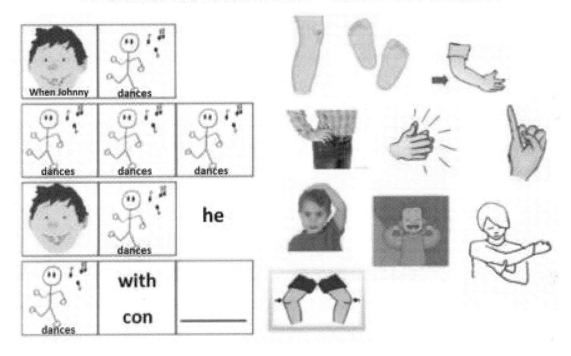

When Little Johnny Dances - Juanito cuando baila

Semantic mapping/graphic organizers

Graphic organizers enable us to introduce new vocabulary so that the student can concentrate on greater linguistic structures. This a great opportunity for students to generate all the vocabulary they know related to a topic. Then we, as educators, can fill in the gap. Using Barefoot Books' *Bear on a Bike* as an example, we can use a graphic organizer to introduce objects related to transportation.

31

 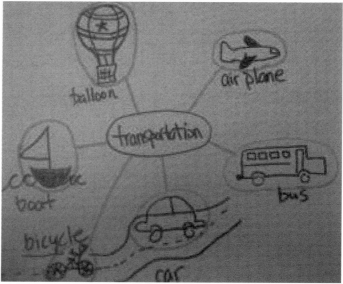

Pre-reading discussion

Pre-reading questions and discussions are designed to tie the students' knowledge, experiences, and ideas to the content of the book. These activities pare well with the graphic organizers. Sticking with the example above, questions can include: How do you get to school? How do your parents get to work? Have you ever been on a bike/plane/boat?

Illustration discussion

What we know about children who are not generating rich language is that their utterances lack detail. Drawing, writing, and painting is a way to have a child actively engage in describing an object or vocabulary topic. Students who have no experience with drawing or writing can participate in group drawing where you draw on a table-size piece of paper and everyone contributes. The student creates a story using illustrations from the selected book. Scaffolding techniques may be used to facilitate higher semantic and syntactic complexity.

Sound production practice

Literacy-based intervention isn't just for language disorders. Articulation targets can be copied out of the book or highlighted. This allows opportunities for specific teaching of certain sound productions prior to generalizing the word or sound into the context of a story.

When the story is eventually read, the student will know that it is her role to read or say all of the words that contain her sound. Here is an example from a Clifford book for a student that is working on /r/ and /l/ at the word level.

T-Bone lay on his back

"I'm full," said Cleo, who had a very big tummy.

"Me, too," said T-Bone, who had an even bigger tummy.

"Me three," said Clifford.

Who had the biggest tummy of all!

Are you ready to open the book? Chances are your students are over-the-top excited to read the book at this point. You can see that this is already a small victory. If you engage in pre-reading activities you have built the foundation on which the story can be enjoyed, absorbed, and replicated.

SLP Confession

"THERE ARE OTHER WAYS TO ADDRESS ARTIC. GIVE A STUDENT POST-ITS AND HAVE HIM WRITE DOWN WORDS THAT INCLUDE SOUNDS HE IS WORKING ON, OR DO A WORD-SEARCH BEFORE READING."

Now it is time to dive in!

3. Book-Reading Activities

Section 5 is dedicated to all the templates that can be reproduced and used in your speech groups. We wanted to take some time and also talk about a few therapeutic strategies that will get your sessions rocking and help your students stay engaged and fly through their goals.

Rock your Therapy with Scaffolding Strategies

Two types of people should read this section:

1. If you are new(er) to speech pathology you can implement the following strategies in any therapy session and enjoy a level of success that only experience normally allows.

2. If you are experienced you probably already incorporate scaffolding techniques into your therapy. However, your *teachers* need to know how you get your students to rapidly add sounds, use new words, and increase communication. Each student responds well to different strategies. If we identify which technique a child likes, our teachers can perform the same magic in their class.

First, a little background on the research behind scaffolding strategies and then on to definitions and a data chart for you to use with each student.

What are scaffolding strategies?

Scaffolding is support provided in a creative and adaptive manner that enables the student to learn the skills at the most independent level possible. Each student has a range of skill levels from what he or she is able to do without any assistance to what he or she is able to do with maximal assistance. This range was termed the Zone of Proximal Development (ZPD) by Vygotsky (1980). The bottom of the zone represents what students can do by themselves and the top of the zone represents what students can do with a lot of help from an adult. As students learn, their zone moves to higher levels. Scaffolding strategies allow an educator to work at a level that is beneficial to each student. Numerous types of scaffolding strategies can be used to help students internalize new information and scaffolding can be used before, during, and after storybook reading.

Scaffolding strategies can be used in shared reading to approach intervention goals at a student's level. Students with language impairments tend to be passive learners (Rabidoux and MacDonald, 2000). Shared reading allows adults to use scaffolding techniques to engage students, allowing them a comfortable way to be active in the learning process, during intervention, in the classroom, and in the home. There is strong support in the literature indicating that students who are active in the learning process learn more quickly and retain information better (Feldman and Denti, 2004).

The Best Scaffolding Strategies

Print reference

The educator references a target from the book by pointing or commenting (e.g. The educator points to an illustration and asks, "What is happening in the picture?")

Cloze procedures

The educator provides the first part of an utterance and the student completes the thought (e.g.

E: Goldilocks tried the porridge of the small bear and it *was*…. S: just right).

Syntactic and semantic expansions

The educator expands on an utterance provided by the student using the grammar and vocabulary

targets (e.g. S: Goldilocks asleep. E: Yes, Goldilocks is asleep in the little bear's bed.).

Comprehension questions

The educator asks the student a question targeting an appropriate level of complexity for the student

(E: Why do you think Goldilocks ate the little bear's porridge? S: It was just the right temperature.).

Binary choice

The educator offers the student two choices of responses (e.g. E: Whose chair did Goldilocks break?

Was it the little bear's chair or the papa bear's chair? S: The little bear's chair.).

Modeling

The educator models the target structure for the student (e.g. E: What happened when the bears got

home from their walk? They found all the things Goldilocks had used.)

Scaffolding Strategies Data Chart

Here is a chart of strategies that can be used to take data on your students' responsiveness to

different types of scaffolding. Share these results with parents and educators on the student's team.

Scaffolding Strategy	Response and Example
Modeling (show)	
Print reference (picture cues)	
Expansions (add to sentence)	
Binary choice (give 2 choices)	
Cloze procedure (fill in the blank)	
Comprehension questions	

Brain-Based Learning Strategies

Brain-based learning strategies incorporate **movement, music, stress reduction, multisensory strategies,** and **changes of state** to maximize learning (Jensen, 2009). What is the commonality among these? These techniques are powerful, often easily implemented, and can be utilized during lessons to rapidly move children toward reaching their goals.

As a topic that began in the 1980's, brain-based research has taught us that brains are capable of learning new processes. This means that we can *always* support positive changes for our clients and students. Regardless of background experiences, influences of second language needs, and personality, all individuals are capable of learning. We acknowledge that each individual is unique; however, all brains have natural responses to certain events. For example:

- learning does not take place when stressors are high
- neurons and synapses are activated when multi-sensory strategies are used
- brains learn better when trust and rapport are built

As you read the template and game-making sections, you will see that specific brain-based strategies are recommended for many activities. Remember, *how* you do something makes as much of an impact as *what* you're doing. The recommended strategies will outline steps for energetic and engaging action items that will result in more effective learning retention.

What does brain-based learning look like?

Truth be told, it looks like fun! Instead of sitting around a horseshoe-shaped table and rehearsing the parts of the story, your students will be hopping across the floor from one picture of a story grammar component to the next. Instead of asking your student about the characters in a story, he will be playing hand jive games with a peer to support his memory of key storybook characters. Instead of rushing into data collection and interventions, educators will take the time to build rapport and trust. With the aforementioned goals obtained, students will work harder and have a collaborative relationship in which to obtain support and motivation for success with their goals. And, they will know that they are capable of building 'bigger, smarter brains.' This is a term we use in our brain-based learning that students start to identify with as they make tangible improvements.

Here is a list of frequently used brain-based strategies. You can read their explanations here or see videos of each strategy at: http://bilinguistics.com/brain-based-learning/

Brain-Based Strategies

Syllable Slap	Instruct one child to put her palms up and another child to lightly slap the other child's palms, 1 time per syllable, while both practice saying the target word.
Reenact the Story	Have the children reenact the story, acting out the different characters and action words from the story (e.g. heaved, pulled, found). They can also reenact other sequences and concepts addressed in the story. Example: Plant a seed: Instruct the children to squat down, swivel their feet, and pretend to make a hole. Jump into the hole and say, "Seed!" Grow by placing their arms by their sides and slowly stand while saying, "Stem." Extend arms and yell, "Leaves!"
Story Grammar Jump	Print off the visuals for the different story elements. Lay them out on the floor (like a hopscotch board) OR draw the story elements on butcher paper as a group. Have each child jump from 1 story grammar element to the next and explain each one.
Music	Music is a core component of brain-based learning due to its direct access to the auditory cortex and inclusion of movement. Play calming or upbeat music (depending on your children) and do one of the following activities: Move to a different corner of the room, pass a ball, or play musical chairs.
Gross Motor Movement	Kinesthetic movement increases the positive effects of brain-based learning. Have children jump, clap, give high fives, or any other fun gross motor movement to correspond with the number of animals, number of syllables in a word, or number of words in a sentence.
Review Goals	Have students incorporate music into knowing their goals. For example: "I work" (clap clap), "I work" (clap clap), "I work on ... (telling stories)!

HOW TO USE STORYBOOKS

Using Literacy....Without Books

We have had the opportunity to talk about books to our fellow SLP-peers. And due to a myriad of reasons, there may not be an opportunity to find an appropriate book for a therapy session. Here's the thing, literacy and stories exist everywhere—whether you have a book in front of you or not. Here are a few examples of how to work on story grammar components without an actual book. Remember, SLPs are MacGyvers. We can make a story out of a few coins, some pocket lint and a tongue depressor.

Student Experience: Sometimes when you pick up a student, he is excitedly talking about an event that happened in his life. We use these opportunities (and excitement!) to create a story.

SLP Experience: Students enjoy hearing stories about their SLPs. So, tell them about your favorite childhood memory.

Video: We can all agree that children love watching television and using electronic devices. With the advent of short videos in the last decade, our students and clients can recount videos they have viewed. "Miss, it was this dad hiding in a bear costume and scaring his family!" These short videos also have all of the story grammar components. Capitalize on this moment, and use it to teach literacy concepts!

SLP Confession

"IT WAS TIME FOR ME TO SEE A GROUP OF 2ND AND 3RD GRADE STUDENTS WORKING ON LANGUAGE. MY IEP MEETING RAN OVER AND I DIDN'T HAVE TIME TO GRAB A BOOK FROM THE LIBRARY. WITH A WHITE BOARD AND A FEW DRY ERASE MARKERS IN HAND, I STARTED TELLING THEM A STORY ABOUT MY FAMILY'S JOURNEY TO AMERICA.

MY MOUTH TOLD FAMILIAR WORDS THAT MY MOM ONCE TOLD ME, AND MY HANDS DREW MEDIOCRE PICTURES OF MY PARENTS' LIFE EVENTS. I WAS SHOCKED AT HOW MUCH THEY ATTENDED TO THE STORY, AND A WEEK LATER, A PARENT TRACKED ME DOWN TO TALK ABOUT HER SON'S EXCITEMENT."

Movie: Remember, favorite movies are a great way to work in literacy skills. With the internet, you can also find visuals from the movie to work on different language goals (e.g., sequencing, describing). You can also have the students create different versions of their favorite movie, have them add a character, create a different ending, or retell the movie in a different location.

Middle School Literacy-Based Intervention - Focus on Non-Fiction

Middle school has really high expectations when it comes to a student comprehending what they are learning and answering questions.

Students need to extrapolate meaning from text to make predictions, identify critical features of a problem (who's involved, how it's solved, dangerous or not) and identify critical features of an interaction (who, relationship, positive or negative).

The problem is that many of our middle school students with impairments are still lacking the foundational abilities to answer questions that would normally be acquired in elementary school. Secondly, core comprehension skills were primarily taught through fictional stories, while middle school content is built around non-fiction.

How do we bridge this gap and intervene with appropriate

grade-level materials?

Non-fiction Literacy-Based Intervention

Storybooks have long been used as educational tools. They provide a structure for teaching concepts while keeping the student engaged and interested. Story structure additionally assists in retention and retrieval of classroom concepts due to familiarity with stories, repetition, and formulaic patterns. The benefits of literacy-based intervention can be transferred over to non-fiction by making the following modifications.

Step 1: Use Non-fiction but continue to paint a vivid story

One way to dramatically cut down on your therapy planning is to have your students bring their homework to your group. This can be math-word problems or pretty much anything from language arts. Non-fiction is often boring to students. Read the homework and then recast the story with vivid imagery.

"I don't know what you see but in my brain, I see an older man sitting on a dock, sweating, and trying to hall in the biggest fish with the news camera right behind him on the grass."

The movie that you help create in your students' minds (this is describing skills, SLPs!) will give them the backdrop to refer to when answering questions. Imagery gives students a powerful way to retrieve information. And do you know how popular you will be with your students and teachers if their homework improves?

Step 2: Obtain Better Wrong Answers

The receptive language concern that we hear most often from teachers is: "My student can't answer questions." If we rely on this RIGHT/WRONG model we are ignoring crucial data that will be our students' bridge to correct responses. We need to take data on whether their "wrong" answer is in the right ballpark. For example, if you ask a student a *where* question, their answer should be a *place*. If you ask a student a *who* question, their answer should be a *person or character*.

My first group each Tuesday is two boys. When asked: "What month is it?" One said his birthday month and the other said "blue." Obviously, there are better wrong answers. Getting them in the right answer group moves them closer to the correct answers.

Step 3: Teach Answers to Questions in Groups

Answers to questions can be categorized just like vocabulary. Build an entire wall or book of possible answers to the four main questions (WHO, WHAT, WHEN, WHERE). You can provide random answers that a student matches to the group without even asking the question! *"When"* questions are particularly difficult because they come in specific sets (e.g. 7 days of the week, 4 seasons, 12 months), are not easy to visualize (What does Tuesday look like?), and rely on verb tense (When will he…, When did he…, When is he going to…?).

Step 4: Use Visuals

What is the biggest difference between fiction and non-fiction literature? No pictures. When children initially gain their comprehension abilities they are taking in visual, auditory, and often tactile cues. In middle school, we abandon this for plain text and maybe one grainy black-and-white image at the top. Reintroduce visual stimuli from the groups of answers you created in Step 3.

Here is an example: I was working with a middle school student on his story retelling skills. I used Flying Lessons and Other Stories, a compilation of short stories written for 8-12 year-olds by diverse authors (edited by Ellen Oh). I started reading, and my student, a child in the Life Skills class, did not appear engaged with the non-fiction story presented in the forward. I admit that the reading level surpassed his level of understanding, but I wanted to give him access to age-appropriate books. Finally, Tony said, "I don't like *Flying Lessons* because no pictures." I'm glad he conveyed his message, and we (easily) made pictures to support his understanding. Of course, I didn't have the storybook template I typically use. So, a sheet of paper, a line drawing of four quadrants and some mediocre drawing on my part did the trick. With the visuals, Tony enjoyed the story and retold the story with the characters, setting, problem, feelings, and a solution.

Ellen Oh found her dream pet in a mangy cat found on the streets. She carried him home hoping her parents and apartment complex would change their minds on the No Pets rule. The short journey earned her scratches all over her body, swollen eyes, protruding welts and the discovery of a feline allergy.

WHO-WHAT-WHERE-WHEN Visuals

The following four WH-question visuals were put together by Maria Mitidieri, a bilingual speech pathologist working at the middle school level. Print these off to support your older students. You can download color copies for free from our Speech Therapy Materials Page:

https://bilinguistics.com/speech-therapy-materials/

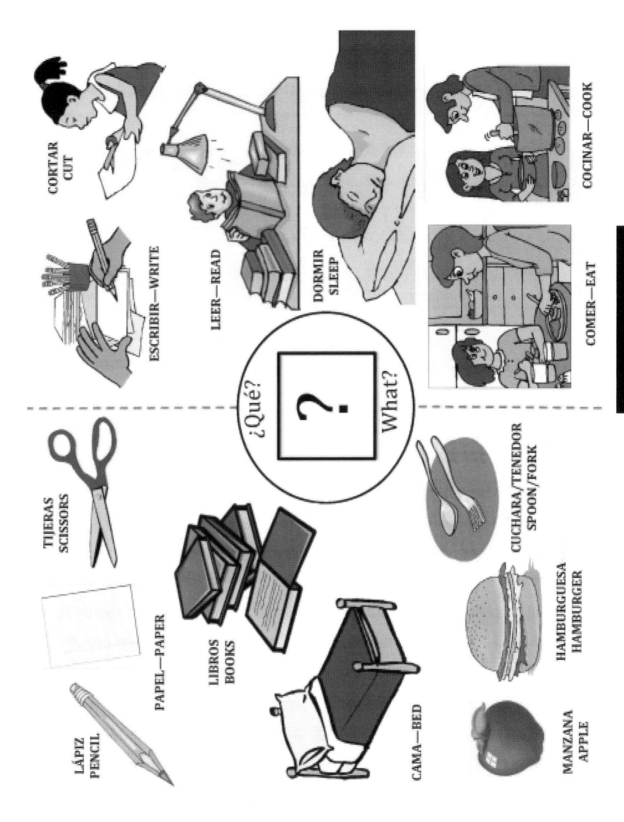

CORTAR — CUT

ESCRIBIR — WRITE

LEER — READ

DORMIR — SLEEP

COCINAR — COOK

COMER — EAT

¿Qué?

?

What?

TIJERAS — SCISSORS

PAPEL — PAPER

LIBROS — BOOKS

LÁPIZ — PENCIL

CAMA — BED

CUCHARA/TENEDOR — SPOON/FORK

HAMBURGUESA — HAMBURGER

MANZANA — APPLE

Developed by Maria Mitidieri, M.A., CCC-SLP. Color version available on our Speech Therapy Materials Page:
https://bilinguistics.com/speech-therapy-materials/

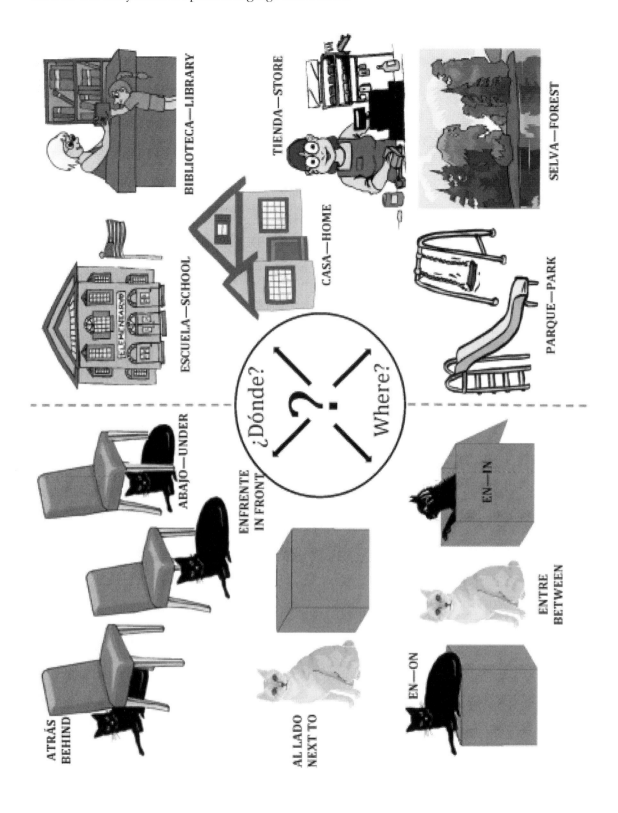

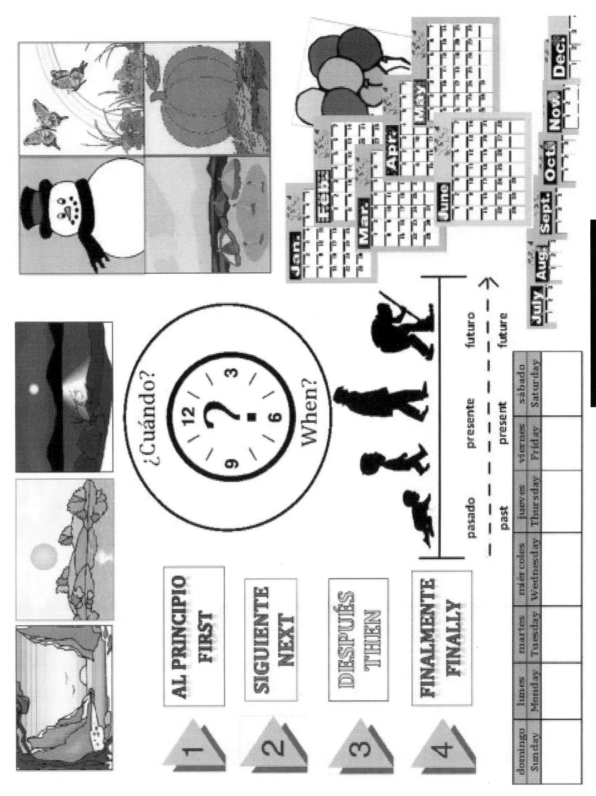

Developed by Maria Mitidieri, M.A., CCC-SLP. Color version available on our Speech Therapy Materials Page:
https://bilinguistics.com/speech-therapy-materials/

Narrative Development - Parts of a Story

Students benefit academically when they bridge the gap between a story and the narrative components. These components are taught in Kindergarten and by 3rd – 5th grade students are annotating stories, writing original pieces and being judged for complexity. Eventually they are tested on narrative aspects.

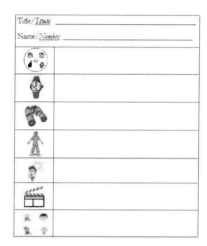

Pretty high-level stuff, right? We laminate the materials in this section and display them in our classrooms. We have additionally created a story grammar rap that is fun and helps the students remember.

Working on story grammar is a great way to align to the curriculum. Secondly, kids are three times as likely to remember when gestures are involved. Yes, THREE TIMES! You can see a video of the Story Grammar Rap here: https://bilinguistics.com/speech-therapy-video-tip-story-grammar-rap/

Materials: cardstock, laminating paper, scissors, Velcro

Instructions:

- Print out the following page for your students.
- Print out the pages of narrative components and cards on cardstock or laminate.
- Print out the blank boxes and attach Velcro to the squares and to the back of the cards.
- Make sets for group therapy: This activity will work with any book and is extremely effective in group therapy. Save time by making a set of 3 or 4 right away.

Suggestions for use:

- Have the child put the story elements in the order in which they occurred in the story (note: the order of story elements may change based on the story).
- Have the child draw or write out the story element, using the visual cues (ex. Write, "The turnip was gigantic" next to the picture for "Problem").
- Retell the story using the visual representations for story elements.
- Use these visuals to have the child reproduce the story rap.
- Use these visuals to check for story comprehension while asking questions.
- Print out copies of the visuals and use them to play a game or review story elements.

Story Recall, Sequencing, and Narrative Components
Recontar un cuento, secuencia y las partes narrativas

Title/*Título*: _____

Name/*Nombre*: _____

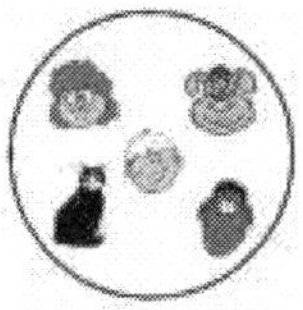

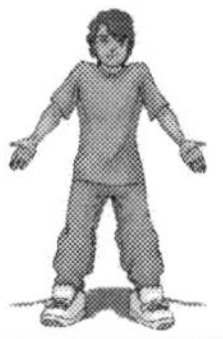

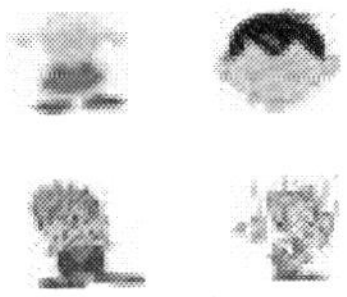

HOW TO USE STOYBOOKS

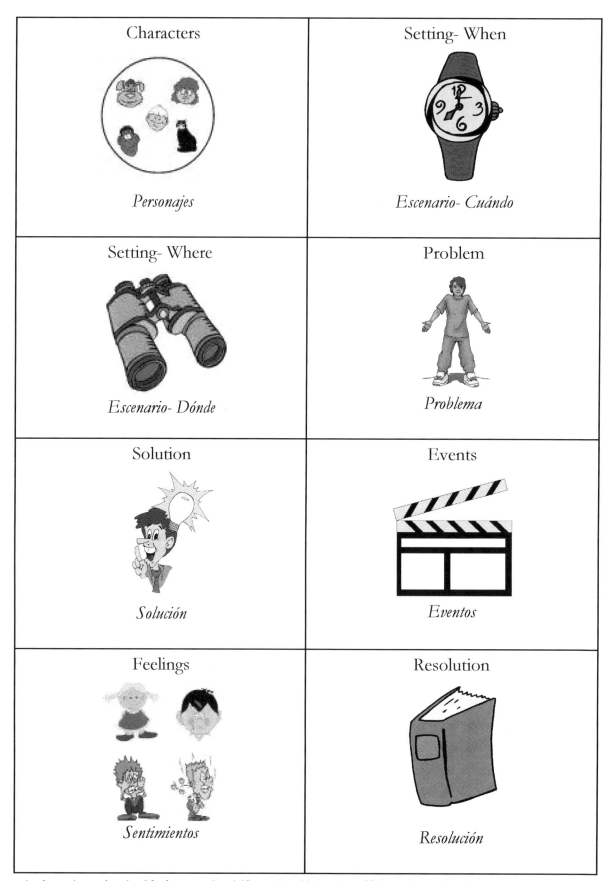

Characters	Setting- When
Personajes	*Escenario- Cuándo*
Setting- Where	Problem
Escenario- Dónde	*Problema*
Solution	Events
Solución	*Eventos*
Feelings	Resolution
Sentimientos	*Resolución*

Parts of a Story and Story Grammar Rap Visuals

Characters

The characters are the people in a story, in a story.

Setting

Setting is **when** and **where**, **when** and **where**.

Problem

Problem, hey what's wrong? Uh oh!

Solution / Plan

Solution, make a **plan,** make a **plan**!

Events

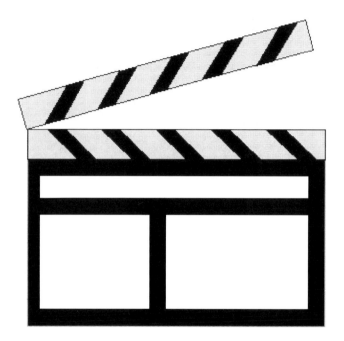

Events- 3, 2, 1, **Action!**

First

Then

Next

After that

Feelings

Feeling, how do you feel, do you feel?

Happy? Sad? Scared? Or mad?

Resolution

Apoyo visual para el rap del cuento

Personajes

Los personajes son las **personas** en el cuento, en el

cuento.

Escenario

Escenario, dónde y cuándo, dónde y cuándo.

Problema

Problema, ¿Qué pasó? ¡Ay no!

Solución / Plan

Solución, hacer un **plan,** hacer un **plan**!

Eventos

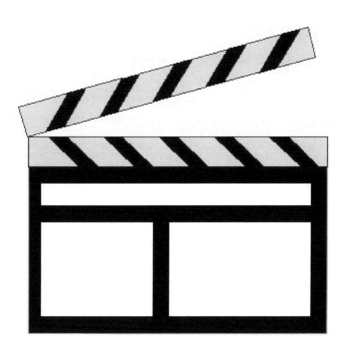

Eventos- 3, 2, 1, **Acción**!

Primero

Luego

Entonces

Después

Sentimiento

Sentimiento, ¿Cómo está, cómo está? ¿Feliz? ¿Triste?

¿Asustado? ¿O enojado?

Resolución

In Summary: Here are some quick tips for effectively running your speech therapy sessions.

Thirty minutes can be the fastest time interval if you have planned for it or the slowest if you didn't have time to put a speech therapy session together effectively. In the first few weeks of school for example, we have not established our routine and you can bet that the students haven't either. Rely heavily on the library, book discovery, and a keen, concise schedule to get all of your groups humming along and achieving classroom objectives as they go.

Book Discovery: Expressive Language (7 minutes)

Place a large number of books on a topic around the table. Encourage students to freely pick any book, look through it, comment, trade, and show friends what they see. Tell them they have 2 minutes and at the end let them choose one book that you look through (non-fiction) or read (fiction). This gives you an idea as to how familiar they are with the topic.

Speech Therapy Session Activity Set-up: Receptive Language (8 minutes)

Empower and challenge students by having them set up for the activity. Explain what they will be doing, show an example, and then ask for helpers to gather crayons, paper, glue, etc. Increase the level of difficulty in each speech therapy session by including numbers, an instruction, an order to the instruction, and descriptions of the materials.

Speech Therapy Session Activity: Expressive Language (18-20 minutes)

Hone in on specific communication goals by working together and then targeting individual student's goals while the others are finishing minor tasks. Rely heavily on successful students to demonstrate to friends how to say a sound, follow instructions, or complete a task.

Post-Activity Review (clean up, homework): Receptive Language (8 minutes)

Ask the initial helpers to gather and return the materials they brought. Have each student stand, present his work, say something about it, and carry it to their backpack, folder, or cubbie. Reward a student for returning a signed parent letter to encourage communication and interaction with the family.

4. Post-Reading Activities – After the Book is Closed

The story is over after the last page, right? What could possibly be left? Students with speech-language impairment rarely get to answer questions correctly and don't often know the answers like their always-ambitious classmates. At this point, they have finally heard a story that they understand and can talk about. Post-reading activities give them a chance to demonstrate their knowledge, in a language-rich manner, and share in front of their peers. This has the added benefit of boosting their confidence. Moreover, if you choose a book that they are reading in class, you can share what you have been working on with teachers so that they can call on your students too and give them another opportunity to demonstrate their knowledge.

Great Post-Reading Activities

Discussion questions

The post-reading timeframe offers us the opportunity to share our opinion. Having an opinion requires prior knowledge of an event or circumstance. Having an opinion is also empowering. Children are not always given the option to state whether they like or do not like an activity. It is completely fair for a child to share that she does not like a story. This also informs your decisions on the next books you choose.

Grammar activities

Stories are most often told in the past tense and in the third person. You have just *finished* the story which gives plenty of opportunities to talk about what the student just read, made, heard, or discussed. It also presents the rare opportunity to rotate between past tense (he wrote) and past progressive forms (he was writing). For your older students, it is a grand opportunity to dive into the conditional tense as each student discusses what he *would* do if he *were* the main character.

Sound practice

Sounds that were targeted throughout the book reading can be added to a success wall or a homework page that is sent home to the parents. We print simple generic parent letters in English and Spanish that say: "This week we have been working on the _____ sound. Practice the following words with your child."

Add the words to the paper or images of the words and send them home. If you have bilingual students, just use pictures and encourage parents to come up with words that include the target sound.

Vocabulary activities

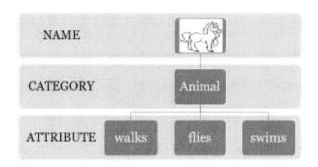

Children remember vocabulary based on their connection to the concept and their experience. Vocabulary is remembered based on how strong our knowledge is about how each object fits into our world. The name of an object (e.g. horse) is more readily retrieved from our memory when we know what group it pertains to (category: animals), what it looks like (attributes: four legs, a main, tall), and what it is for (function: you ride it, it works on a farm). Vocabulary activities can be used to strengthen a student's knowledge related to the vocabulary that was introduced in the book because the information can be found in the settings, actions, and descriptions of the stories. These activities build vocabulary and strengthen recall.

Narrative retelling

Narrative retelling is the real test of a mastered skill. This is also the easiest of the post-reading activities. Each student gets a turn to be the teacher. This can happen each day or once per book. They get to sit in your chair, wear your name badge, and tell everyone what to do. They are given the book and are expected to tell the story without reading and show the illustrations that correspond

SLP Confession

"MY STUDENTS LOVE ACTING OUT THE STORY AND IT IS AN ACTIVE WAY TO WORK ON THEIR RE-TELLING. THEN WE SHOWCASE TO THEIR PEERS. I EVEN GOT PARENT CONSENT AND COORDINATED WITH ANOTHER SLP TO HAVE OUR GROUPS SKYPE TO EACH OTHER WHAT THEY CREATED."

with what they are saying.

Conclusion

In the same way that we began this section, we want to reiterate that with literacy-based intervention we are not necessarily doing anything new.

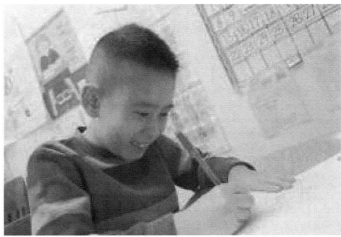

1) We are now planning effectively because now we know that if we use academic topics the students will have more opportunities to use the language we are building. We are also thinking about what is going home to mom and dad because the child now has the language to have a meaningful conversation about what they did that day.

2) The *old you* opened the storybook immediately. The *new you* knows that culture, language and SES cause students to show up with different types of knowledge. The new you will not make any assumptions and will instead teach about the book's topic before the topic begins. The new you also feels super savvy because you just performed an extra week of therapy with ZERO planning.

3) The book-reading portion used to be 100% of your therapy. It is still the largest part but is now based on the structure of the narrative so that the child can transfer these abilities to any story or communication that he undertakes outside of your speech session. You know that we are not in the business of teaching content. That is what general education is for. We are building the linguistic structure for that content to hang on.

4) The old you snapped the book shut and ushered students back to class. The new you knows that children with impairments need higher levels of repetition and might need and want the book repeated. This might also be the first time that they successfully understood a story. The new you is going to ask comprehension questions to make their confidence explode, build and play games related to the narrative structure, and write similar, yet-new stories based on the content they just absorbed. And, because you have been so brave and so thorough, you have gained the right to enter speech pathology's sacred ground: inferencing questions such as WHY and HOW, identifying critical features of a problem (who's involved, how it's solved, dangerous or not), identifying critical features of an interaction (who, relationship, positive or negative), and novel story creation. Basically, you get to introduce the ability set that is right on the border of "within normal limits."

4. Assessing What to Work on, Choosing Goals, and Taking Data

Our speech pathology team is very successful at treating and dismissing children even when they come from different cultures or lower socio-economic brackets. If you were to ask us why, it is in large part due to taking goal writing and progress monitoring very seriously. It makes sense at a certain level, doesn't it? If you are trying to fix a problem and you are working exactly on what is broken, you have a high likelihood of success? Conversely, if you are working in a general area with no way to measure results, how successful will you be? Despite this fact, many graduates come out of their master's programs lacking confidence in their ability to perform informal assessment, choose goals, and effectively taking data. We want this section to change how *you* relate to goals, your data, and the success of your caseload.

Are you off course?

Airplane flying provides a great metaphor for us as we talk about goals and collect data. An airplane that flies

one degree off course will miss its target by one mile for every 60 miles flown. This means that an airplane leaving L.A. for New York with a 1 degree error will be 40 miles off course by the time it gets to the East Coast. Would this be acceptable to you if you were on this airplane? Of course not! Secondly, autopilot settings are needed to constantly make corrections as the plane flies along. Micro-adjustments need to be made due to changes in wind-speed and the curvature of the earth. Do you think that evaluating the progress of a student is valuable if it only happens every 12 months?

What we need is effective method to make sure that we are "on course" from the very beginning. And because we are human and children mature, we need a way to check our progress along the way. In this section, we will start by showing you an easy way to evaluate the narrative abilities of a child so that you have a baseline. We will then talk about writing great goals and introduce you to an online goal bank in English and Spanish from which you can choose goals. We will conclude by talking about better ways to ensure good data collection.

Assessment of Fictional Narratives

Story-telling and our ability to understand a simple narrative are the building blocks of our communication. When we are answering questions in school, recounting an event in our lives, or explaining the steps in a process, we are telling a story. The person who is listening to us has expectations that the story will be in a certain order and contain important information. We can therefore test a child's ability to share information and understand what is happening around them based on their ability to create a narrative. In the last half of this book, you will also see that story narratives are also our inroads to teach grammatical structures and communication abilities.

Gathering a Language Sample

The first step to helping a child is finding out what a child knows so that we can celebrate her strengths and know what is absent so that we can build upon it. We gather data to identify what elements are present in a child's narrative and what might be missing. First, it is important to take at least two samples. A topic that is unfamiliar or of low interest might elicit a poor sample. By collecting two independent stories we can be sure that we have an accurate representation of a child's knowledge (Klecan-Aker and Brueggeman,1991). Secondly, prior to asking the child to tell a story, we need to provide a model. Research shows that asking a child to tell a story without a model does not provide a true indication of their narrative ability (Klecan-Aker, McIngvale and Swank, 1987).

Use a Wordless Picture Book

Narrative abilities are most easily captured by using a wordless picture book so that the student is not intimidated or influenced by reading. Almost any wordless picture book will work. Mercer Meyer has a series of "frog books" which have no text and a relatively simple plot line with lots of action and emotion. For the truly research minded, a database based on these books has been created of children from English and Spanish speaking cultures as well as many other backgrounds.

Record the story as it is being told and type at the same time

Many of us are still scarred by our experience taking language samples in grad school. What we are proposing here is a much less painful process. Use your phone to record while the child is telling the story. Audacity (http://www.audacityteam.org/download/) is also free downloadable program for your computer that makes recording and splicing easy. While you are recording, don't just sit back with your coffee as the child is telling the story. For most children younger than 3rd grade, you can capture most of the story as they are speaking if you type along.

Analyze the story

Now that you have the language sample, what do you do? You need to analyze the macro-structure (big picture) and micro-structure (details of a story). We have created this cheat sheet of the different aspects of stories with developmental expectations.

Assessment of Fictional Narratives (page 1 of 2)

Name: _____ Date: _____ DOB: _____ C.A.: _____

Macrostructure (Overall Organization of Story)

Age of Acquisition	Universal Expectancies	Expectancies That May Vary Due to Culture

By: 3 years	☐ Setting
	  ☐ Time
	  ☐ Place
	☐ Initiating event	

4yrs		☐ Temporal sequence ☐ Central theme
5yrs	☐ Labels characters ☐ Labels surroundings ☐ Attempts ☐ Consequence ☐ Reaction	
6yrs	☐ Provides implicit aims/intentions of characters ☐ Resolution	
7yrs		☐ Theme and moral
8yrs	☐ Explicit aims/plans of characters (uses words like "decided to")	
11yrs	☐ Multiple plans ☐ Multiple attempts ☐ Multiple consequences	☐ Embedded Stories
>12yrs	☐ Two separate but parallel episodes that influence each other	

Glenn and Stein (1980); Hedberg and Westby (1993); Liles (1987); Stein (1988); Hudson, Shapiro, McCabe, and Peterson (1991)

A downloadable version is available on our Evaluation Resources Page: https://bilinguistics.com/evaluation-resources/

Assessment of Fictional Narratives (page 2 of 2)

Microstructure (Grammaticality and Cohesive Devices):

SEMANTICS (word knowledge):

☐ **Nouns**: variety, age-appropriate, specific
☐ **Pronouns**: gender, correct part of speech
☐ **Verbs**: variety, age-appropriate, specific, appropriate tense selection
☐ **Adjectives and Adverbs**: variety, age-appropriate, specific

Comments:_____

_____.

MORPHOLOGY (word structure):

☐ **Plurals**: regular and irregular
☐ **Articles**: agree in number and gender
☐ **Verbs**: subject/verb agreement; appropriate tense conjugations
   o Regular
   o Irregular

Comments:_____

_____.

SYNTAX (sentence structure):

Utterance Length
Sentence Complexity

☐ simple sentences
☐ compound sentences (i.e., DEPENDENT CLAUSE+ DEPENDENT CLAUSE connected with *and, or, but*)
☐ complex sentences (i.e., DEPENDENT CLAUSE+ INDEPENDENT CLAUSE connected with *but, so, when*, etc.)
☐ Conjunctions used:_____

Grammaticality of sentences

☐ Are sentences complete and grammatical/do they contain all obligatory words

Comments/Observations:_____

_____.

SOCIAL/PRAGMATICS:

☐ Does child make story appropriate for audience?
☐ Does child provide appropriate amount of information for listener?
☐ Do they stay on task/topic?
   Comments/Observations:_____

_____.

A downloadable version is available on our Evaluation Resources Page: https://bilinguistics.com/evaluation-resources/

KNOWING WHAT TO WORK ON

Detailed case study and example of language sampling

Let's take a look at a 7-year-old student who qualifies for language therapy. We gathered language samples from conversation, story-telling without an example, and story-telling after he heard an example. He is bilingual so we gathered samples in both languages. What you see below is *way* more work than you will need to do for children who have already qualified. We wanted to illustrate how much linguistically-rich information that we can gather in a short amount of time.

<u>Josepi, Age 7;2 Qualified for Speech Services with an Expressive and Receptive Impairment</u>

Conversational Language Sample

Informal observations indicated that Josepi's conversational language skills are stronger in Spanish than English. The examiner asked Josepi about what he does at home and who he plays with, and what he received as a gift on a recent holiday. He was able to give basic information in response to "Wh" questions (e.g., who, what, where) but his utterances were limited grammatically.

I have it the move it robot yellow.	This[what did your brothers and sisters get?]My boy little have it the RRRRRRR (driving)
I opened the present the robot.	
Press the body button	My big boy has it the the this one 9drawing)
Now the move (marching in room)	Have it the down up (out of chair marching?)
[what else did you get?]	[did you have a Christmas tree"]
My naneraThe hobbitThe man	Green tree have it green tree beautiful
De de de de happ out here	[do you have a dog?] No, no have it.

Story-telling Exercise (TELL & RETELL)

Josepi was asked to tell a story after looking at pictures in a wordless picture book. An example of Josepi's stories in English are presented here, followed by an explanation:

English storytelling <u>without</u> an example	The where the frog coming for?
Right here the boy the dog the frog	Frog, are you here?
The boy the sleeping.	No.
Here.	Frog, were are you?
The (hi) him boy.	Woof woof woof.

Example Narrative Summary

Three stories were elicited from Josepi. English without a model (example), Spanish without a model, and Spanish with a model.

Josepi's English language sample could be described as naming the characters and using gestures and sound effects to tell the story. His Spanish language samples were more linguistically rich and are considered a truer measure of his language abilities. Josepi's language sample in English was smaller, less complex, and contained more grammatical errors. Some of the errors are typical of Spanish-influenced English but others were not, and are indicative of language impairment.

In Spanish, Josepi was asked to tell a story without a model and at a different time tell a story with a model. There was considerable language growth between the two language samples (tell and retell), which indicates that Josepi benefits greatly from being able to see/hear an example before he is expected to complete a task.

Josepi produced utterances of 1-6 words in Spanish. His utterances included the characters of the story and some actions (sleeping). The story was told from the perspective of the main character as Josepi spoke as though he were the boy. Much of the story contained sound effects and naming of the characters. He mentioned the place (in the water) on a few occasions but typically did not mention the place or used non-specific words (there/here). Without the pictures it would have been difficult to understand what Josepi was talking about.

The story that he generated included verbs in present tense but did not include past or future. He did use certain verbs (cayó/fell) that occur more routinely in the past tense than the present. He did not use adjectives or many conjunctions (and). Without the known context of the book, much of the story would have been difficult to understand due to a lack of content, reduced use of pronouns and articles, and reliance on carrier phrase such as "and…" While his story included the action of many pictures, the story was not unified into a cohesive narrative. He did not use cohesive elements (e.g. "and then") to link the story together.

Grammatically, Josepi struggled to use complete sentences that were grammatically and syntactically correct. He had difficulty including articles and pronouns consistently. Additional syntactic errors included inclusion of extra articles, lack of plurals, missing aux-verb…, use of non-informative naming (it, that, everywhere), and using a different word order.

Can you think of another way to get information this rich?

This language sample gave us a wealth of information about Josepi's expressive language skills and insight into successful strategies for intervention and classroom support. More than anything, if gives us an extremely detailed description of what to focus on in speech therapy and how to write goals.

Writing Incredible Speech Therapy Goals

You have completed your evaluation and it's time to write your report. Or you are sitting in an office/portable/corner of the library trying to decide what to work on. Either way, you have a child who is impaired and you have to make an ethical decision about what will most effectively move her in the direction of typical. In this section, we are going to talk about how to choose and write effective goals, how to connect the goals to the people that care, and how to connect them to the curriculum so they continue to make gains when they are not directly with you.

5 Tips to Write Speech Therapy Goals that Rock

1. Keep the timeline in mind

Remember, we write speech therapy goals to be mastered in a certain amount of time. For those in home-health and clinics, goals typically need to be mastered in 3-6 months. Lack of mastery conveys that efforts were not productive, and reauthorization of speech therapy is denied. For those working in the schools, you need mastery by the end of the IEP-year. Continuing the same goals would show that your efforts have not been successful. So, this is permission to *not* select goals for all weakness demonstrated on the evaluation. Refine your efforts.

2. Determine mutual goals

Before choosing goals, find out what is important to the family. Within a school setting, find out what skills would be valuable for the classroom teacher. Then, look at your assessment results. With input from the child's VIPs, you will be addressing the most meaningful communication needs. For adult clients, get their input and priorities, as well.

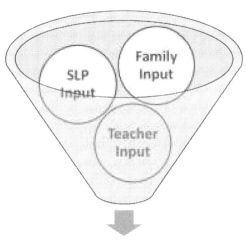

Functional Goals

3. Goals need to be functional

Our goals need to be more functional so that they truly impact our client's day-to-day life. Case in point—I am currently working with a 24-year-old young man. After a few speech therapy sessions, I understood that he is most excited about meal time, creating art, and watching his favorite television shows. His goals involve those exact desires and needs.

4. Goals need to be measurable

As SLPs, we know that it's important to write good, measurable speech therapy goals. But are we really thinking this through or just cutting and pasting? During the last three years, I have had a chance to see tons of speech reports as I travel around the state doing re-evaluations. These IEPs arrive from all over the country. Many reports contain brilliant goals but many simply do not. This has changed my goal-writing-perspective greatly. Here are some sample goals:

Good	Better
Goal 1: Will express wants and needs using a variety of 3-word combinations.	Goal 1: Express wants and needs using a variety of 3-word combinations <u>in 70% of opportunities</u>, **with minimal cues**.
Goal 2: Describe (e.g., color, size) using a variety of 2-3word combinations.	Goal 2: Describe (e.g., color, size) using a variety of 2-3word combinations <u>in 50% of opportunities</u>, **given no cues**.

5. Goals Need to Make an Impact

School professionals can benefit from learning from the clinical folks on this point. Clinic goals are extremely obtainable in a 3-6 month window so that the client can continue to receive services and funding. School professionals, we have to rely on teachers and parents to know what a child is doing academically and what the needs of the home are. These are the environments where your student will be practicing everything that you teach.

And if you don't want to write speech therapy goals yourself, know that we have done it for you in Spanish and English. Check it out at: https://bilinguistics.com/speech-therapy-goals/

SLP IEP Goal Bank

EXPRESSIVE LANGUAGE - Morphology
Will use article/gender agreement [in a structured activity/in conversation]   *Usará los artículos con el género apropiado [en una actividad estructurada/en conversación]*
Will use [#] present progressive-tense verbs in [a phrase/sentence/conversation]   *Usará [#] verbos en el tiempo presente progresivo en [una frase/oraciones/ conversación]*
Will use [regular/irregular] plural markers in [phrase/sentence/conversation]   *Usará el "-s" (ej, perros) y "-es" (arboles) que indican la forma plural en [frases/oraciones/conversación]*
Will use article/number agreement [in a structured activity/inconversation]   *Usará los artículos con el numero apropiado [en una actividad estructurada/en conversación]*
EXPRESSIVE LANGUAGE - Syntax

KNOWING WHAT TO WORK ON

Connecting Teachers, Students, Parents, and Speech Therapy Through Goal Writing

Writing speech therapy goals is a relatively small part of what we do. I wouldn't go as far as to say that they are an afterthought, but they garner a small amount of our attention compared to the amount of time we put into evaluating, writing reports, and conducting therapy. Yet goals, despite their small stature, are the ties that bind together everyone that influences the progress of a child.

Goals help teachers understand the academic impact of communication

We know that our goals are written to support the curriculum. But do our teachers? A teacher's job is to demonstrate learning. If a child answers incorrectly, is it because 1) they do not know 2) or because they can't communicate their knowledge? This is where we come in. When we explain goals to teachers we need to use a big fancy word: "because."

"Chad will follow 2-step directions with minimal cues BECAUSE when you are trying to get him in line and he is running around, it is BECAUSE he can only follow 1-step directions right now."

Students need to know what they are working on

Students can't improve if they don't know what they are working on. It makes them more accountable and if everyone in the group knows, it's a great way to build rapport. Every day, as they enter, clean up, fill in their chart, or get their stickers, students should tell you (in their own words) what they are working on.

Goals tell parents why a child is in speech therapy

Sometimes parents don't understand why a child is in speech therapy. The home environment requires very basic interpersonal communication that is largely repetitious. Academic vocabulary is another story. When we explain goals to parents we need to 1) explain the academic importance and 2) give an example from the home so that the parents can participate.

"John uses single words when he speaks and we want him to say two-words together so he can let Ms. Crosby know when he needs help. At home, if he uses one word, "water" use 2-3 words to give him a bigger example of what to say: "I want water."

We are not required to translate IEP paperwork but parents benefit from reading goals in their home language. Again, check out our Speech Therapy Goal Bank because it is in Spanish and English: https://bilinguistics.com/speech-therapy-goals/.

Finding a fun and effective way for teachers, parents, and students to know their goals is important. You have put a tremendous amount of effort into your evaluation and progress notes. Take one more minute to make sure that everyone understands what you are working on and that your goals are functional, measurable and make and make an impact.

Alignment of State Curriculum and Speech-Language Therapy

An important part of our work as speech-language pathologists is to support children within an educational setting. This is stated in our federal guidelines through the **Individuals with Disabilities Education Act (IDEA)**. Part of our responsibility is to ensure that our efforts support the general education curriculum. Why is this important? It ensures that we are tackling the most salient concepts that result in academic success.

The Law

First, let's talk about the law. The three parts that we need to know are:

1. FAPE: All children need to have a <u>F</u>ree and <u>A</u>ppropriate <u>P</u>ublic <u>E</u>ducation.
2. Access to the General Education: This means that all Individual Education Plans (IEPs) need to align to the general education curriculum.
3. Least Restrictive Environment: Students should be provided special education services in the least restrictive environments.

Because our educational plans need to consider the sentiments of the grade level curriculum, we are required to align them. So, that means that the goals of fourth grader working on his receptive and expressive language goals need to relate to fourth grade state adopted curriculum standards.

Aligning to Curriculum

I promise that this goal is easier to accomplish than one may think. Here is the most important takeaway. We are speech-LANGUAGE pathologists. That means we are the experts in all-things-language. Speech-language therapy is a part of all academic curriculums. So, rest easy. By doing your job, you are likely addressing their curriculum expectations. Here is what you can do:

Talk to Grade Level Teachers:
They can tell you EXACTLY what the standards are for their grade level. Tuck away the information. Voila! You have information for your students for that grade level for the remainder of your career.

Use your state's list or the list we provided below:
Many of our goals already align with the standards for English Language Arts (ELA). I guarantee you will see very similar goals for speech-language therapy. ELA is where we get the most bang out of our time, and we are following the law of the land!

Common Core
Kindergarten

    1. With prompting and support, ask and answer questions about key details in a text.

    2. With prompting and support, retell familiar stories, including key details.

    3. With prompting and support, identify characters, settings, and major events in a story.

First Grade

    1. Ask and answer questions about key details in a text.

    2. Retell stories, including key details, and demonstrate understanding of their central message or lesson.

    3. Describe characters, settings, and major events in a story, using key details.

Second Grade

    1. Ask and answer such questions as who, what, where, when, why, and how to demonstrate understanding of key details in a text.

    2. Recount stories, including fables and folktales from diverse cultures, and determine their central message, lesson, or moral.

    3. Describe how characters in a story respond to major events and challenges.

Third Grade

    1. Ask and answer questions to demonstrate understanding of a text, referring explicitly to the text as the basis for the answers.

    2. Recount stories, including fables, folktales, and myths from diverse cultures; determine the central message, lesson, or moral and explain how it is conveyed through key details in the text.

3. Describe characters in a story (e.g., their traits, motivations, or feelings) and explain how their actions contribute to the sequence of events.

Fourth Grade

1. Refer to details and examples in a text when explaining what the text says explicitly and when drawing inferences from the text.

2. Determine a theme of a story, drama, or poem from details in the text; summarize the text.

3. Describe in depth a character, setting, or event in a story or drama, drawing on specific details in the text (e.g., a character's thoughts, words, or actions).

Fifth Grade

1. Quote accurately from a text when explaining what the text says explicitly and when drawing inferences from the text.

2. Determine a theme of a story, drama, or poem from details in the text, including how characters in a story or drama respond to challenges or how the speaker in a poem reflects upon a topic; summarize the text.

3. Compare and contrast two or more characters, settings, or events in a story or drama, drawing on specific details

Sixth, Seventh, and Eighth Grade

1. Engage effectively in a range of collaborative discussions (one-on-one, in groups, and teacher-led) with diverse partners on grade 6/grade 7/grade 8 topics, texts, and issues, building on others' ideas and expressing their own clearly.

2. Review the key ideas expressed and demonstrate understanding of multiple perspectives through reflection and paraphrasing.

3. Present claims and findings, sequencing ideas logically and using pertinent descriptions, facts, and details to accentuate main ideas or themes; use appropriate eye contact, adequate volume, and clear pronunciation.

4. Determine or clarify the meaning of unknown and multiple-meaning words and phrases based on grade 6 reading and content, choosing flexibly from a range of strategies.

5. Demonstrate understanding of figurative language, word relationships, and nuances in word meanings.

Ninth and Tenth Grade

1. Initiate and participate effectively in a range of collaborative discussions (one-on-one, in groups, and teacher-led) with diverse partners on grades 9-10 topics, texts, and issues, building on others' ideas and expressing their own clearly and persuasively.

a. Propel conversations by posing and responding to questions that relate the current

discussion to broader themes or larger ideas; actively incorporate others into the discussion;

and clarify, verify, or challenge ideas and conclusions.

b. Respond thoughtfully to diverse perspectives, summarize points of agreement and disagreement, and, when warranted, qualify or justify their own views and understanding and make new connections in light of the evidence and reasoning presented.

2. Present information, findings, and supporting evidence clearly, concisely, and logically such that listeners can follow the line of reasoning and the organization, development, substance, and style are appropriate to purpose, audience, and task.

3. Determine or clarify the meaning of unknown and multiple-meaning words and phrases based on *grades 9-10 reading and content*, choosing flexibly from a range of strategies.

4. Demonstrate understanding of figurative language, word relationships, and nuances in word meanings.

Eleventh and Twelfth Grade

1. Initiate and participate effectively in a range of collaborative discussions (one-on-one, in groups, and teacher-led) with diverse partners on grades 11-12 topics, texts, and issues, building on others' ideas and expressing their own clearly and persuasively.

a. Propel conversations by posing and responding to questions that relate the current discussion to broader themes or larger ideas; actively incorporate others into the discussion; and clarify, verify, or challenge ideas and conclusions.

b. Respond thoughtfully to diverse perspectives, summarize points of agreement and disagreement, and, when warranted, qualify or justify their own views and understanding and make new connections in light of the evidence and reasoning presented.

2. Present information, findings, and supporting evidence clearly, concisely, and logically such that listeners can follow the line of reasoning and the organization, development, substance, and style are appropriate to purpose, audience, and task.

3. Determine or clarify the meaning of unknown and multiple-meaning words and phrases based on *grades 11-12 reading and content*, choosing flexibly from a range of strategies.

4. Demonstrate understanding of figurative language, word relationships, and nuances in word meanings.

Texas Essential Knowledge and Skills (TEKS)

A small handful of states have not adopted the common core, Texas being one of them. While the requirements per grade level are largely identical, the order and focus of each area vary a bit. We have included Texas' TEKS related to communication for those of you working in the Lone Star State.

Pre-Kindergarten – Articulation

I.C.3.   Child shows competence in initiating social interactions.

I.C.4.   Child increasingly interacts and communicates with peers to initiate pretend play scenarios that share a common plan and goal.

II.C.1.   Child's speech is understood by both the teacher and other adults in the school.

III.C.3. Child produces the correct sounds for at least 10 letters.

Pre-Kindergarten – Receptive Language

II.A.1. Child shows understanding by responding appropriately.

II.A.2. Child shows understanding by following two-step oral directions and usually follows three-step directions.

II.D.2. Child demonstrates understanding of terms used in the instructional language of the classroom.

Pre-Kindergarten – Expressive Language

II.B.2. Child engages in conversations in appropriate ways.

II.B.3. Child provides appropriate information for various situations.

II.D.1. Child uses a wide variety of words to label and describe people, places, things and actions.

II.E.1. Child typically uses complete sentences of four or more words and grammatical complexity usually with subject, verb, and object order.

II.E.2. Child uses regular and irregular plurals, regular past tense, personal and possessive pronouns, and subject-verb agreement.

II.E.4. Child combines more than one idea using complex sentences.

III.D.2. Child uses information learned from books by describing, relating, categorizing, or comparing and contrasting.

Kindergarten – Articulation

2G. Blend spoken phonemes to form one-syllable words

3A. Identify the common sounds that letters represent

22. Students speak clearly and to the point, using the conventions of language. Students continue to apply earlier standards with greater complexity. Students are expected to share information and ideas by speaking audibly and clearly using the conventions of language.

Kindergarten – Receptive Language

21B. Follow oral directions that involve a short, related sequence of actions

5A. Identify and use words that name actions, directions, positions, sequences, and locations

4B. Ask and respond to questions about texts read aloud

16A. Understand and use the following parts of speech in the context of reading, writing, and speaking (with adult assistance):

    (i)   past and future tenses when speaking

    (ii)   nouns (singular/plural)

    (iii) descriptive words

(iv) prepositions and simple prepositional phrases appropriately when speaking or writing (e.g., in, on, under, over)

(v) pronouns (e.g., I, me)

Kindergarten – Expressive Language

4B. Ask and respond to questions about texts read aloud

5A. Identify and use words that name actions, directions, positions, sequences, and locations

10B. Retell important facts in a text, heard or read

16A. Understand and use the following parts of speech in the context of reading, writing, and speaking (with adult assistance):

(i) past and future tenses when speaking

(ii) nouns (singular/plural)

(iii) descriptive words

(iv) prepositions and simple prepositional phrases appropriately when speaking or writing (e.g., in, on, under, over)

(v) pronouns (e.g., I, me)

16B. Speak in complete sentences to communicate

22. Students speak clearly and to the point, using the conventions of language. Students continue to apply earlier standards with greater complexity. Students are expected to share information and ideas by speaking audibly and clearly using language.

1st Grade – Articulation

2D. Blend spoken phonemes to form one- and two-syllable words, including consonant blends (e.g., spr)

2F. Segment spoken one-syllable words of three to five phonemes into individual phonemes (e.g., splat =/s/p/l/a/t/).

28. Listening and Speaking/Speaking. Students speak clearly and to the point, using the conventions of language. Students continue to apply earlier standards with greater complexity. Students are expected to share information and ideas about the topic under discussion, speaking clearly at an appropriate pace, using language.

1st Grade – Receptive Language

6A. Identify words that name actions (verbs) and words that name persons, places, or things (nouns)

14A. Restate the main idea, heard or read

21B. Follow oral directions that involve a short related sequence of actions

20A. Understand and use the following parts of speech in the context of reading, writing, and speaking:

(i) verbs (past, present, and future)

(ii) nouns (singular/plural, common/proper)

(iii) adjectives (e.g., descriptive: green, tall)

(iv) adverbs (e.g., time: before, next)

(v) prepositions and prepositional phrases

(vi) pronouns (e.g., I, me)

(vii) time-order transition words

27A. Listen attentively to speakers and ask relevant questions to clarify information

27B. Follow, restate, and give oral instructions that involve a short sequence of actions

1st Grade – Expressive Language

4B. Ask relevant questions, seek clarification, and locate facts and details about stories

9A. Describe the plot (problem and solution) and retell a story's beginning, middle, and end with attention to the sequence of events

14A. Restate the main idea, heard or read

19A. Write brief compositions about topics of interest to the student

20B. Speak in complete sentences with correct subject-verb agreement

20A. Understand and use parts of speech in the context of reading, writing, and speaking:

(i) verbs (past, present, and future)

(ii) nouns (singular/plural, common/proper)

(iii) adjectives (e.g., descriptive: green, tall)

(iv) adverbs (e.g., time: before, next)

(v) prepositions and prepositional phrases

(vi) pronouns (e.g., I, me)

(vii) time-order transition words

27A. Listen attentively to speakers and ask relevant questions to clarify information

27B. Follow, restate, and give oral instructions that involve a short sequence of actions

2nd Grade – Articulation

2G. Identify and read at least 300 high-frequency words from a commonly used list

23A. Use phonological knowledge to match sounds to letters to construct unknown words

29. Listening and Speaking/Speaking. Students speak clearly and to the point, using the conventions of language. Students continue to apply earlier standards with greater complexity. Students are expected to share information and ideas that focus on the topic under discussion, speaking clearly at an appropriate pace, using language.

2nd Grade – Receptive Language

5C.   Identify and use common words that are opposite (antonyms) or similar (synonyms) in meaning

14A.   Identify the main idea in a text and distinguish it from the topic

28A.   Listen attentively to speakers and ask relevant questions to clarify information

28B.   Follow, restate, and give oral instructions that involve a short, related actions

2nd Grade – Expressive Language

3B.   Ask relevant questions, seek clarification, and locate facts and details about stories and other texts and support answers with evidence from text

5C.   Identify and use common words that are opposite (antonyms) or similar (synonyms) in meaning

14C.   Describe the order of events or ideas in a text

17D.   Edit drafts for grammar, punctuation, and spelling using a teacher-developed rubric

28A.   Listen attentively to speakers and ask relevant questions to clarify information

28B.   Follow, restate, and give oral instructions that involve a short, related actions

21A.   Understand and use the following parts of speech in the context of reading, writing, and speaking:

    (i)   verbs (past, present, and future)

    (ii)   nouns (singular/plural, common/proper)

    (iii)   adjectives (e.g., descriptive: old, wonderful; articles: a, an, the)

    (iv)   adverbs (e.g., time: before, next; manner: carefully, beautifully)

    (v)   prepositions and prepositional phrases

    (vi)   pronouns (e.g., he, him)

    (vii)   time-order transition words

    21B.   Use complete sentences with correct subject-verb agreement

29.   Listening and Speaking/Speaking. Students speak clearly and to the point, using the conventions of language. Students continue to apply earlier standards with greater complexity. Students are expected to share information and ideas that focus on the topic under discussion, speaking clearly at an appropriate pace, using of language.

3rd Grade – Articulation

1A.   Decode multisyllabic words in context and independent of context by applying common spelling patterns

30.   Listening and Speaking/Speaking. Students speak clearly and to the point, using the conventions of language. Students continue to apply earlier standards with greater complexity. Students are expected to speak coherently about the topic under

discussion, employing eye contact, speaking rate, volume, enunciation, and the conventions of language to communicate ideas effectively.

3rd Grade – Receptive Language

4C.   Identify and use antonyms, synonyms, homographs, and homophones

5A.   Paraphrase the themes and supporting details of fables, legends, myths, or stories

8A.   Sequence and summarize plot's main events and explain the influence on future events

29A.   Listen attentively to speakers, ask relevant questions, and make pertinent comments

29B.   Follow, restate, and give oral instructions that involve a series of related action

3rd Grade – Expressive Language

2B.   Ask relevant questions, seek clarification, and locate facts and details about stories and other texts and support answers with evidence from text

5A.   Paraphrase the themes and supporting details of fables, legends, myths, or stories

8A.   Sequence and summarize plot's main events and explain the influence on future events

17D.   Edit drafts for grammar, mechanics, and spelling using a teacher-developed rubric

22A.   Use and understand the function of the following parts of speech in the context of reading, writing, and speaking:

(i)   verbs (past, present, and future)

(ii)   nouns (singular/plural, common/proper)

(iii)   adjectives (e.g., descriptive: wooden, rectangular; limiting: this, that; articles: a, an)

(iv)   adverbs (e.g., time: before, next; manner: carefully, beautifully)

(v)   prepositions and prepositional phrases

(vi)   possessive pronouns (e.g., his, hers, theirs)

(vii)   coordinating conjunctions (e.g., and, or, but)

(viii)   time-order transition words and transitions that indicate a conclusion

22C.   Use complete simple and compound sentences with correct subject-verb agreement

29A.   Listen attentively to speakers, ask relevant questions, and make pertinent comments

29B.   Follow, restate, and give oral instructions that involve a series of related of action

30.   Listening and Speaking/Speaking. Students speak clearly and to the point, using the conventions of language. Students continue to apply earlier standards with greater complexity. Students are expected to speak coherently about the topic under discussion, employing eye contact, speaking rate, volume, enunciation, and the conventions of language to communicate ideas effectively.

4th Grade – Articulation

28.   Listening and Speaking/Speaking. Students speak clearly and to the point, using the conventions of language. Students continue to apply earlier standards with greater

KNOWING WHAT TO WORK ON

complexity. Students are expected to express an opinion supported by accurate information, employing eye contact, speaking rate, volume, and enunciation, and the conventions of language to communicate ideas effectively.

4th Grade – Receptive Language

2B. Use the context of the sentence (e.g., in-sentence example or definition) to determine the meaning of unfamiliar words or multiple meaning words

6A. Sequence and summarize plot's main events and explain the influence on future events

11A. Summarize the main idea and supporting details in text in ways that maintain meaning

11D. Use multiple text features (e.g., guide words, topic and concluding sentences) to gain an overview of the contents of text and to locate information

13A. Determine the sequence of activities needed to carry out a procedure (e.g., recipes)

24C. Take simple notes and sort evidence into provided categories or an organizer

27A. Listen attentively to speakers, ask relevant questions, and make pertinent comments

27B. Follow, restate, and give oral instructions that involve a series of related action

4th Grade – Expressive Language

2C. Complete analogies using knowledge of antonyms and synonyms

6A. Sequence and summarize plot's main events and explain the influence on future events

11A. Summarize the main idea and supporting details in text in ways that maintain meaning

11C. Describe explicit and implicit relationships among ideas in texts organized by cause-and-effect, sequence, or comparison

15C. Revise drafts for coherence, organization, use of simple and compound sentences

15D. Edit drafts for grammar, mechanics, and spelling using a teacher-developed rubric

20A. Use and understand the function of the following parts of speech in the context of reading, writing, and speaking:

   (i)   verbs (irregular verbs)

   (ii)   nouns (singular/plural, common/proper)

   (iii)   adjectives (e.g., descriptive, including purpose: sleeping bag, frying pan) and their comparative and superlative forms (e.g., fast, faster, fastest)

   (iv)   adverbs (e.g., frequency: usually, sometimes; intensity: almost, a lot)

   (v)   prepositions and prepositional phrases to convey location, time, direction, or to provide details

   (vi)   reflexive pronouns (e.g., myself, ourselves)

   (vii)   correlative conjunctions (e.g., either/or, neither/nor)

   (viii)   use time-order transition words and transitions that indicate a conclusion

20C. Use complete simple and compound sentences with correct subject-verb agreement

27B. Follow, restate, and give oral instructions that involve a series of related actions

5th Grade – Articulation

28. Listening and Speaking/Speaking. Students speak clearly and to the point, using the conventions of language. Students continue to apply earlier standards with greater complexity. Students are expected to give organized presentations employing eye contact, speaking rate, volume, enunciation, natural gestures, and conventions of language to communicate ideas effectively.

5th Grade – Receptive Language

2B. Use context (e.g., in-sentence restatement) to determine or clarify the meaning of unfamiliar or multiple meaning words

11A. Summarize the main ideas and supporting details in a text in ways that maintain meaning and logical order

11D. Use multiple text features and graphics to gain an overview of the contents of text and to locate information

12B. Recognize exaggerated, contradictory, or misleading statements in text

27A. Listen to and interpret a speaker's messages (both verbal and nonverbal) and ask questions to clarify the speaker's purpose or perspective

27B. Follow, restate, and give oral instructions that include multiple action steps

5th Grade – Expressive Language

2C. Produce analogies with known antonyms and synonyms

11A. Summarize the main ideas and supporting details in a text in ways that maintain meaning and logical order

15D. Edit drafts for grammar, mechanics, and spelling

20A. Use and understand the function of the following parts of speech in the context of reading, writing, and speaking:

   (i) verbs (irregular verbs and active voice)

   (ii) collective nouns (e.g., class, public)

   (iii) adjectives (e.g., descriptive, including origins: French windows, American cars) and their comparative and superlative forms (e.g., good, better, best)

   (iv) adverbs (e.g., frequency: usually, sometimes; intensity: almost, a lot)

   (v) prepositions and prepositional phrases to convey location, time, direction, or to provide details

   (vi) indefinite pronouns (e.g., all, both, nothing, anything)

   (vii) subordinating conjunctions (e.g., while, because, although, if)

   (viii) transitional words (e.g., also, therefore)

20C. Use complete simple and compound sentences with correct subject-verb agreement

27B. Follow, restate, and give oral instructions that include multiple action steps

6th Grade – Articulation

21. Oral and Written Conventions/Spelling. Students spell correctly

6th Grade – Receptive & Expressive Language

2B. Use context (e.g., cause and effect or compare and contrast organizational text structures) to determine or clarify meaning of unfamiliar or multiple meaning words

6A. Summarize the elements of plot development (e.g., rising action, turning point, climax, falling action, denouement) in various works of fiction.

4-12. Reading/Comprehension of Various form of Literary Text (e.g., Nonfiction, Expository, Persuasive). Students understand, make inferences and draw conclusions about the varied structural patterns and features of literary nonfiction and provide evidence from text to support their understanding. Students are expected to identify the literary language and devices used in memoirs and personal narratives and compare their characteristics with those of an autobiography

19A. Use and understand the function of the following parts of speech in the context of reading, writing, and speaking:

(i) verbs (irregular verbs and active and passive voice);

(ii) non-count nouns (e.g., rice, paper);

(iii) predicate adjectives (She is intelligent.) and their comparative and superlative forms (e.g., many, more, most);

(iv) conjunctive adverbs (e.g., consequently, furthermore, indeed);

(v) prepositions and prepositional phrases to convey location, time, direction, or to provide details;

(vi) indefinite pronouns (e.g., all, both, nothing, anything);

(vii) subordinating conjunctions (e.g., while, because, although, if); and

(viii) transitional words and phrases that demonstrate an understanding of the function of the transition related to the organization of the writing

26B. Follow and give oral instructions that include multiple action steps

7th Grade – Articulation

21. Oral and Written Conventions/Spelling. Students spell correctly. Students are expected to spell correctly, including using various resources to determine and check correct spellings

7th Grade – Receptive & Expressive Language

2B. Use context (e.g., cause and effect or compare and contrast organizational text structures) to determine or clarify the meaning of unfamiliar or multiple meaning words

6A. Explain the influence of the setting on plot development for fiction

6B. Analyze the development of the plot through the internal and external responses of the characters, including their motivations and conflicts; and

6C. Analyze different forms of point of view, including first-person, third-person omniscient, and third-person limited.

10A. Evaluate a summary of the original text for accuracy of the main ideas, supporting details, and overall meaning;

10B. Distinguish factual claims from commonplace assertions and opinions

10C. Use different organizational patterns as guides for summarizing and forming an overview of different kinds of expository text

10D. Synthesize and make logical connections between ideas within a text and across two or three texts representing similar or different genres, and support findings with evidence

4-12. Reading/Comprehension of Various form of Literary Text (e.g., Poetry, Nonfiction, Expository, Persuasive). Students understand, make inferences and draw conclusions about the varied structural patterns and features of literary nonfiction and provide evidence from text to support their understanding. Students are expected to identify the literary language and devices used in memoirs and personal narratives and compare their characteristics with those of an autobiography

19A. use and understand the function of the following parts of speech in the context of reading, writing, and speaking:

(i) verbs (irregular verbs and active and passive voice)

(ii) non-count nouns (e.g., rice, paper)

(iii) predicate adjectives (She is intelligent.) and their comparative and superlative forms (e.g., many, more, most)

(iv) conjunctive adverbs (e.g., consequently, furthermore, indeed)

(v) prepositions and prepositional phrases to convey location, time, direction, or to provide details

(vi) indefinite pronouns (e.g., all, both, nothing, anything)

(vii) subordinating conjunctions (e.g., while, because, although, if)

(viii) transitional words and phrases that demonstrate an understanding of the function of the transition related to the organization of the writing

26B. Follow and give oral instructions that include multiple action steps

8th Grade Articulation

21. Oral and Written Conventions/Spelling. Students spell correctly

8th Grade Receptive & Expressive Language

2B. Use context (e.g., cause and effect or compare and contrast organizational text) to determine or clarify the meaning of unfamiliar or multiple meaning words

6A. Explain the influence of the setting on plot development for fiction

6B. Analyze the development of the plot through the internal and external responses of the characters, including their motivations and conflicts

6C. Analyze different forms of point of view, including first-person, third-person omniscient, and third-person limited

10A. Evaluate a summary of the original text for accuracy of the main ideas, supporting details, and overall meaning for expository text

10B. Distinguish factual claims from assertions and opinions for expository text

10C. Use different organizational patterns as guides for summarizing and forming an overview of different kinds of expository text for expository text

10D. Synthesize and make logical connections between ideas within a text and across two or three texts representing similar or different genres, and support those findings with textual evidence for expository text

4-12. Reading/Comprehension of Various form of Literary Text (e.g., Poetry, Nonfiction, Expository, Persuasive). Students understand, make inferences and draw conclusions about the varied structural patterns and features of literary nonfiction and provide evidence from text to support their understanding. Students are expected to identify the literary language and devices used in memoirs and personal narratives and compare their characteristics with those of an autobiography

19A. Use and understand the function of the following parts of speech in the context of reading, writing, and speaking:

(i) verbs (perfect and progressive tenses)

(v) subordinating conjunctions (e.g., because, since)

9th Grade/English I – Articulation

19. Oral and Written Conventions/Spelling. Students spell correctly

9th Grade/English I – Receptive & Expressive Language

2-10. Reading/Comprehension of Various Types of Text (e.g., Expository, Poetry). Students analyze, make inferences and draw conclusions and provide evidence from the text to support their understanding

9. Reading/Comprehension of Informational Text/Expository Text. Students analyze, make inferences and draw conclusions about expository text and provide evidence from text to support their understanding. Students are expected to:

A. Summarize text and distinguish between summaries that capturemain ideas and elements of a text and a critique that takes a position and expresses an opinion

B. Differentiate between text opinions that are substantiated and unsubstantiated

C. Make subtle inferences and draw complex conclusions about the ideas in text and their organizational patterns

D. Synthesize and make logical connections between ideas and details in several texts selected to reflect a range of viewpoints on the same topic and support those findings with textual evidence

11A. Analyze the clarity of the objective(s) of procedural text (e.g., consider reading instructions for software, warranties, consumer publications)

24A. Listen responsively to a speaker by taking notes that summarize, synthesize, or highlight the speaker's ideas for critical reflection and by asking questions related to the content for clarification and elaboration

24B. Follow and give complex oral instructions to perform specific tasks, answer questions, solve problems, and complete processes

KNOWING WHAT TO WORK ON

24C. Evaluate the effectiveness of a speaker's main and supporting ideas

25. Listening and Speaking/Speaking. Students speak clearly and to the point, using the conventions of language. Students will continue to apply earlier standards with greater complexity. Students are expected to give presentations using informal, formal, and technical language effectively to meet the needs of audience, purpose, and occasion, employing eye contact, speaking rate (e.g., pauses for effect), volume, enunciation, purposeful gestures, and conventions of language to communicate ideas effectively

26. Listening and Speaking/Teamwork. Students work productively with others in teams. Students will continue to apply earlier standards with greater complexity. Students are expected to participate productively in teams, building on the ideas of others, contributing relevant information, developing a plan for consensus-building, and setting ground rules for decision-making

10th Grade/English II – Articulation

19. Oral and Written Conventions/Spelling. Students spell correctly

10th Grade/English II – Receptive & Expressive Language

2-10. Reading/Comprehension of Various Types of Text (e.g., Expository, Poetry). Students analyze, make inferences and draw conclusions and provide evidence from the text to support their understanding

9. Reading/Comprehension of Informational Text/Expository Text. Students analyze, make inferences and draw conclusions about expository text and provide evidence from text to support their understanding. Students are expected to:

A. Summarize text and distinguish between a summary that captures main ideas and elements of a text and a critique that takes expresses opinion

B. Differentiate between opinions that are substantiated and unsubstantiated

C. Make subtle inferences and draw complex conclusions about the ideas in text

D. synthesize and make logical connections between ideas and details in several texts selected to reflect a range of viewpoints on the same topic and support those findings with textual evidence

11A. Analyze the clarity of the objective(s) of procedural text (e.g., consider reading instructions for software, warranties, consumer publications)

24A.   Listen responsively to a speaker by taking notes that summarize, synthesize, or highlight the speaker's ideas for critical reflection and by asking questions related to the content for clarification and elaboration

24B.   Follow and give complex oral instructions to perform specific tasks, answer questions, solve problems, and complete processes

24C.   Evaluate the effectiveness of a speaker's main and supporting ideas

25.   Listening and Speaking/Speaking. Students speak clearly and to the point, using the conventions of language. Students will continue to apply earlier standards with greater complexity. Students are expected to give presentations using informal, formal, and technical language effectively to meet the needs of audience, purpose, and occasion, employing eye contact, speaking rate (e.g., pauses for effect), volume, enunciation, purposeful gestures, and conventions of language to communicate ideas

26.   Listening and Speaking/Teamwork. Students work productively with others in teams. Students will continue to apply earlier standards with greater complexity. Students are expected to participate productively in teams, building on the ideas of others, contributing relevant information, developing a plan for consensus-building, and setting ground rules for decision-making

11ᵗʰ Grade/English III – Articulation

19.   Oral and Written Conventions/Spelling. Students spell correctly

11ᵗʰ Grade/English III – Receptive & Expressive Language

2-11.   Reading/Comprehension of Various Types of Text (e.g., Expository, Poetry). Students analyze, make inferences and draw conclusions and provide evidence from the text to support their understanding

9A.   Summarize a text in a manner that captures the author's viewpoint, its main ideas, and its elements without taking a position or expressing an opinion

9B.   Distinguish between inductive and deductive reasoning and analyze these elements in texts and the different ways conclusions are supported

9C.   Make and defend subtle inferences and complex conclusions about the ideas in text

9D.   Synthesize ideas and make logical connections (e.g., thematic links, author analyses) between and among multiple texts representing similar or different genres and technical sources and support those findings with textual evidence

11A.   Evaluate the logic of the sequence of information presented in text (e.g., product support material, contracts)

17A.   Use and understand the function of different types of clauses and phrases (e.g., adjectival, noun, adverbial clauses and phrases

(25)   Listening and Speaking/Speaking. Students speak clearly and to the point, using the conventions of language. Students will continue to apply earlier standards with greater complexity. Students are expected to give a formal presentation that exhibits a logical structure, smooth transitions, accurate evidence, well-chosen details, and rhetorical devices, and that employs eye contact, speaking rate (e.g., pauses for effect), volume, enunciation, purposeful gestures, and conventions of language to communicate ideas effectively

(26)   Listening and Speaking/Teamwork. Students work productively with others in teams. Students will continue to apply earlier standards with greater complexity. Students are expected to participate productively in teams, offering ideas or judgments that are purposeful in moving the team towards goals, asking relevant and insightful questions, tolerating a range of positions and ambiguity in decision-making, and evaluating the work of the group based on agreed-upon criteria

12th Grade/English IV – Articulation

19.   Oral and Written Conventions/Spelling. Students spell correctly

12th Grade/English IV – Receptive & Expressive Language

2-10.   Reading/Comprehension of Various Types of Text (e.g., Expository, Poetry). Students analyze, make inferences and draw conclusions and provide evidence from the text to support their understanding

11A.   Reading/Comprehension of Informational Text/Procedural Texts. Students understand how to glean and use information in procedural texts and documents

17A.   Use and understand the function of different types of clauses and phrases (e.g., adjectival, noun, adverbial clauses and phrases

25.   Listening and Speaking/Speaking. Students speak clearly and to the point, using the conventions of language. Students will continue to apply earlier standards with greater complexity. Students are expected to formulate sound arguments by using elements of classical speeches (e.g., introduction, first and second transitions, body, and conclusion), the art of persuasion, rhetorical devices, eye contact, speaking rate (e.g., pauses for effect), volume, enunciation, purposeful gestures, and conventions of language to communicate ideas effectively

26.   Listening and Speaking/Teamwork. Students work productively with others in teams. Students will continue to apply earlier standards with greater complexity. Students are expected to participate productively in teams, offering ideas or judgments that are purposeful in moving the team towards goals, asking relevant and insightful questions, tolerating a range of positions and ambiguity in decision-making, and evaluating the work of the group based on agreed-upon criteria

KNOWING WHAT TO WORK ON

Better Speech Therapy Data Collection

Why does data tracking make us so nervous? We asked fellow SLPs, and it boils down to two main reasons:

Getting it Done: Data tracking is hard because you are trying to do it in real time. Your brain is going in many directions, and it's a lot of work.

Taking GOOD Data: We need speech therapy data collection to be continual to make sure we can measure the child's progress. What does *good* data tracking look like? It has to be measurable. This sounds easy, but we all know that many factors contribute to the challenges of data-keeping: students' behavior, level of cuing, chosen activity, etc.

Here are four ways to improve your data collection and a special focus taking data on how well a student follows directions. We then conclude this section by showing how to evaluate your therapy materials to make sur that they are addressing the goals of your students and clients.

1. Let students take their own data

Students of any age can mark their own progress. During articulation work, they can put a checkmark, star, or sticker in a box. Language therapy groups can mark if they answer a question, count the words in their utterances, or count parts of sentences that are in the right sequence. Be really savvy about it and have their data counting be in groups of 10 so that you can get percentages immediately. Here are some examples from articulation groups.

- Students put a check on a piece of paper when they say a sound as we go around the table.
- Students find /s/, /r/, and /l/ sounds in the book we just read. They say the words and give themselves a check.
- Students use iconic phonology pages with 10 boxes under each picture and make their own checks.
- Students use a counter to track their number of repetitions per word while I track the level of cuing.

2. Make it explicit

Taking data should not be a secret affair. First, your students should know his goals. Second, he should know that our tally marks represent when he "finds his sound" or "answers a question" correctly. This makes progress happen faster! It is feedback for our students.

3. Take *good* data less often

It is impossible to take good data constantly during every session. Here are various data-taking schedules. Find what works for you:

"I take the first few minutes of each session to collect data on a set number of trials. Then the rest of the session can be spent on the activity without the worry of collecting data."

"I take data for 1-2 students per session rather than tracking of all students in the group. "

"I usually get good hard data on goals once per month per student."

4. Talk and share with your fellow SLPs

Each situation, district, or company has certain requirements for data. Make sure to talk to your peers about how they are collecting data. Guaranteed, you are not alone in trying to take data effectively. Talking to your peers will help you arrive at a system that works well for you. Here are a few examples to use to get yourself started.

Date:	Activity:											%
Name	Objective #1											
	Objective #2											

(Right margin vertical text: KNOWING WHAT TO WORK ON)

Quickly Improve Data for Following Directions

Educational plans often include goals that target understanding simple directions. A child needs to follow directions for her own safety as well as to reduce frustration. Unfortunately, children most frequently hear rapidly-fired commands in situations that demand an immediate response. These situations do not provide visual support and offer little time for teaching. While this is a necessary part of life for many students, other opportunities are needed to practice following directions in a more controlled setting. The events

that take place throughout the day offer multiple chances to show a child how to properly follow directions. Most children enjoy participating in daily activities but can grow frustrated if they cannot participate or produce good work because they cannot follow directions.

Your plan to quickly improve how you collect speech therapy following directions data

Directions can be easily described as having a number of 1) steps and 2) components. Our instructions increase in difficulty as one or both of these aspects increase in number. Look at this chart below. You can see steady growth of an instruction as you add components.

	1 Step	2 Steps	3 Steps
0 Components	Sit (or) Stand up	Stand up and get in line	Stand up, get in line, and don't move
1 Component	Touch your nose	Start walking and stop at the water fountain	Stop working, get in line and put on your coat
2 Components	Give me the blue square	Walk with your hands behind your back and stop in the hall	Stop working, put your things in your backpack, and get in line
3 Components	Touch the big red circle (from a group of red or big things)	Go to your table and sit in the yellow chair	Put your stuff in your desk, go to the door, and walk silently down the hall

Make a copy of this chart and observe a student in a handful of settings to see where he is having the most success and where he is having difficulty. Once you know his level of functioning, share the information with his teacher to make her life easier and the child more successful. We then chose to increase his average performance by adding one step or one component. Count your tick marks in these boxes to serve as your data collection.

We identify where the child is functioning and share that with the teacher. We then increase complexity (below move over or down one box) until the child demonstrates difficulty. Use the chart below or collect your own data in a similar fashion.

Do your therapy materials address your goals?

This question almost sounds silly but the truth is that not everything we do in speech therapy addresses our goals very well. True, some activities are magical and can be used in almost any situation. But how do we know? We need to evaluate our therapy materials and decide whether they address the goals we are working on. If they do not, we can add things to our therapy sessions or abandon them all together.

As an example, I had a book that I loved and that the students loved to work with. This book make many of my therapy sessions fly (*Where the Wild Things Are*). I had another book that I loved that completely stunk as far as speech therapy went and I was always trying to find ways to make my therapy better (*The Gift of Nothing*). The truth was that the good book inherently addressed therapy goals better due to the sequence of the story, the variety of words, and high concentration of articulation sounds. The other book was just cute. Chances are, what works best for you is also therapy-rich. We can evaluate everything that we use in therapy to know how richly it supports our goals and efforts. Use the chart on the following page to remind you what to work on and whether an activity is good or not. A word of warning, sadly you might have to ditch some of your favorites.

Both through the American Speech Language Hearing Association (ASHA) Schools Surveys and through surveys that we have conducted through The Speech Therapy Blog, we see professionals continually beat themselves up for not being able to take good data. They worry about not providing great therapy for the same reason because they are overwhelmed. Hopefully by now you see that what you choose to work on (goals) and what you measure (data) are one and the same. I think that we have traditionally treated this as two different processes.

Secondly, we are also guilty of seeing data collection as something that is painful or something that interferes with intervention. Hopefully, you also see that the children can take their own data and that their work *is* data collection. You just need the right templates and materials so that what they

99

create can be easily counted and quantified. This next section has dozens of reproducible templates for you to use in your therapy. Keeping with the spirit of this book, we are going to tell you *how* to use them so that great therapy, progress, and data collection can all happen seamlessly.

	Activity 1:	Activity 2:
Speech		
Phonological Awareness		
Labeling		
Similarities/Differences		
Describing		
Categorizing		
Sequencing		
Following Directions		
Asking & Answering ?s		
Utterance Expansion		
Article/Noun Agreement		
Prepositions		

5. Literacy Based Intervention Templates

The following pages contain blank versions of graphic organizers, explanations, and examples for how to successfully use templates for literacy-based intervention. It is important that we take a moment and explain really how simplistic this is. Those of us who are successful with literacy-based intervention, those of us that boost academic productivity, are not doing something other-worldly.

Quite the opposite. We have copies of a small number of highly-impactful templates that can be used with any book. My car trunk and my workbag are no longer packed with junk. Some days yes. But most of the 36 weeks that I am working in the schools, I am carrying one book, a handful of materials, and binder of blank templates.

You work with children who have impairments, or at the very least, are not functioning at the same level as their peers.

You have two choices:

1) Teach them how to tell a story or talk about a specific topic.

2) Teach them a structure on which they can talk about anything or tell any story…independently...when you are not there.

Not much of a choice, is it?

Especially not if you work in Special Education. What SPECIAL Education means to me is that a child learns in a way that is different than most of his peers. His brain has different priorities and is organized in different ways in which GENERAL education is not set up to support. You know this to be true because he is on your caseload with a report saying that General Education isn't fully supporting his needs.

Therefore, the topic that you teach can change as much as you want. But the process, the way in which the child accesses the topic, HAS TO REMAIN THE SAME.

Use these templates for a while and a child will begin to understand what is expected of him. He will gain the internal mental structure that he will hang his communication on.

Are you ready? Let's start with two quick goal charts and then we are going to deep dive into the two templates that are the cornerstone for our success.

Storybook Activity Goal Chart

This table provides a list of the most common communication goals. Use this list to think about and explain how different activities can be used to address different goals.

	Activity 1: _____	Activity 2: _____	Activity 3: _____
Speech			
Phonological Awareness			
Labeling			
Similarities / Differences			
Categorizing / Describing			
Sequencing			
Following Directions			
Asking and Answering ?s			
Sentence Expansion			
Article/Noun Agreement			
Prepositions			

Tabla de objetivos de las actividades del cuento

Esta tabla contiene una lista de los objetivos de comunicación más comunes. Utilice esta lista para explicar cómo las diferentes actividades se pueden utilizar para hacer frente a diferentes objetivos.

	Actividad 1:	Actividad 2:	Actividad 3:
Habla			
Conciencia fonológica			
Nombrar			
Semejanzas / Diferencias			
Categorías / Describir			
Hacer secuencias			
Seguir instrucciones			
Contesar y hacer preguntas			
Expandir oraciones			
Concordancia de articulo y nombre			
Preposiciones			

Multi-Part Story-Telling

At what point do we dismiss students from Special Education? Or, if I asked you to define what a robust story was, what would it include?

Let's start by defining what a ROBUST is:

- It is minimally a 4-part story
- Each "part" is content-rich containing "who, what, where, and when" information
- It is in the right sequence/order
- It uses cohesive elements (first, then, after, at the end)
- It uses long, grammatically-rich sentences.

If you are doing the math, that is 16 pieces:

Four "WH" question content pieces X four parts. There are also four cohesive elements (first, then, after, at the end) but those sometimes define the "when" content.

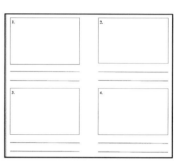

How satisfied would you be, and would your teachers be, if your students were producing 16-part narratives that included all major content pieces, in the right order? Let's walk through how to use this four-part graphic organizer to get us there.

Discourse in Speech Therapy

First, the heavy stuff:

As a clinical tool, discourse analysis has great potential for deferentially diagnosing a variety of clinical populations and making predictions about the impact of language disorders on communication in real-life situations. Hatch (1992) asserts that narrative discourse is the most universal discourse genre, as all cultures have storytelling traditions. Ulatowska and colleagues have documented that personal narratives relating a "frightening experience" tend to result in dramatic and lengthy discourse in Caucasian and African-American subjects (Ulatowska and Olness, 2001).

Now, the fun stuff:

If we take our professorial bow-tie off, what we are really saying is that we are looking for a way to get a child to INDEPENDENTLY combine all the small parts of language into something big and pretty.

A Complete Discourse Example

Let's start by taking a look at the end goal and then talk about getting there. Success means that a child:

- Draws four pictures from the story in the correct sequence
- Writes minimally four sentences, one per picture
- Starts each sentence with one cohesive element (first, then, after, at the end)
- Produces content in each sentence that can answer WHO, WHAT, WHEN, WHERE
- Has a way to double-check his or her work
- Knows what is missing and can correct it
- Knows how to evaluate a peer's work and offer constructive ways to improve.

Here is an example in Spanish for *"How the Grinch Stole Christmas."* The pictures are drawn first. Then the sentences are written. WHO, WHAT, WHEN, WHERE are written from memory on the side of the page. WHO, WHAT, WHEN, WHERE are circled in distinct colors. Each story-part is studied to make sure it has 1 WHO, 1 WHAT, 1 WHERE, and 1 WHEN.

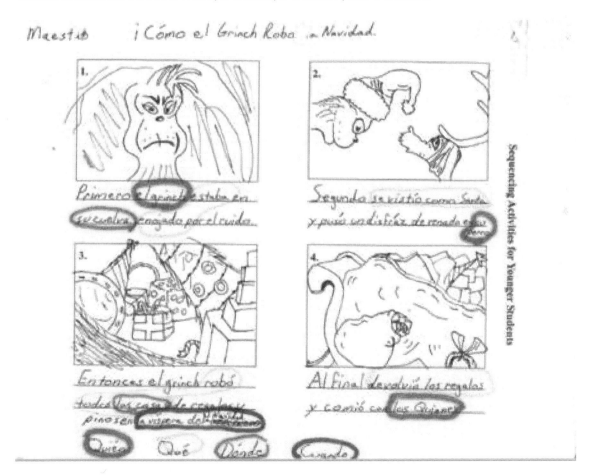

Building Story-Telling Abilities

So how do we get there? In order to teach a child to produce such a dramatically complex story, we have to break the story down into its components, teach the components, and then sew it back together. If you have students who are high functioning, go ahead and start with the 4-Part Story-Telling Template. If they are younger, more impaired, or have holes in their story, take a detour with me through three activities and then we will arrive back at the 4-part story. We first need to know how to:

- Sequence and use cohesive elements
- Answer "WH" questions

Sequencing and Use of Cohesive Elements

Regardless of age, most children rapidly learn how to put a story in the right order. Further, most students use some form of cohesive elements. Typically, it is saying "and" while they are thinking of what to say next. Some use "and then" to start every single sentence. When students do not sequence story events or use cohesive elements, it is often something that they simply need to learn.

Sequencing

We first need to know whether a child can sequence. The easiest way to do this is to photocopy 4 pictures out of your storybook. Put them on the table and ask the student to put them in the right order. If they get it correct, move on. If they are not in the right order, teach the child how to use the book to check his work. REMEMBER, our end goal is independence. Teach them how to open the book and check their work. Yes, you can buy sequencing cards in box sets. But how does a child using these sets know if he is right or wrong? He can't unless you tell him. Use a book and he can figure it out on his own. This is empowerment!

Cohesive Elements

On the front end, I am pretty strict about using FIRST-THEN-AFTER-(AT) THE END (PRIMERO-LUEGO-DESPUÉS-AL FINAL). Students can add more elements such as "afterwards" or put them in a different order eventually. However, we are after consistency, high repetition, and a minimally-viable story to begin with.

If I have a group that cannot successfully use cohesive elements, we abandon the books for a week and focus solely on learning these four words. I put 4 pieces of tape on the floor outside of my office and we jump chanting FIRST-THEN-AFTER-THE END in unison.

Marrying Sequencing and Cohesive Elements

Sequencing and cohesive elements are two sides of the same coin. One is the demonstration of knowledge of the sequence (receptive language). The other is communicating the sequence through specific words (expressive language). On the lowest level and with your youngest clients or students, print out the four words and print out four pictures. Have the student place the pictures above the words. Have her check the book for correctness or allow group members to use the book and cue their friends when they have placed a picture correctly.

| FIRST | THEN | AFTER | THE END |

A word of warning, use "first" but stay away from ordinal numbering words (second, third…). Ordinal numbering allows the student to blindly repeat a word without thinking about story order. It is equivalent to the child who can sing the alphabet but can't identify any letters.

For young students, you will write these out every time and have them repeat you before they tell you the sentence that goes along with the picture. (SLP) "First…" (Student) "First, he went to the car."

Asking and Answering "WH" Questions

Asking and answering questions is the other two-sided coin you need in your lit-based money purse. A child answering WHO-WHAT-WHEN-WHERE questions by pointing or speaking is demonstrating his receptive language abilities and ensuring comprehension. A story that contains WHO-WHAT-WHEN-WHERE information is the smallest-yet-richest expression of language. We all tell stories in sentences every day. When we leave one of these four components out, our listening partner is forced to ask for the missing information:

"Today I went out to lunch with Nancy." Where did you go?"

Learning how to answer "WH" Questions

What we are going to start with sounds simplistic. But again, if you don't know what your student is missing, this is a mini-evaluation of sorts. If your students have no trouble answering questions, jump ahead. But I have found that most of students with language impaired are representative of what is found in the following research. Here are two snapshots concerning the difficulties some children with language disorders have with asking and answering 'Wh' questions.

In comparison with normal children within the same chronological age range, the children with language impairment were not only less successful in producing answers which adhered to the informational category constraints of the particular wh-form but also provided fewer responses characterized by fact, logic, and credibility (Parnell, Amerman, and Harting, 1986).

Deficits in the ability to ask and answer questions have a serious impact on students' development of communication, classroom performance, and on the development of reading comprehension (Wilson, Fox, and Pascoe, 2012).

Introduce "WH" Questions

Introduce the questions by telling them that there you will focus on four different types, by naming them, by writing them, or even by choosing them from a list of words. Successful students can tell you what the most important questions are that they have to answer and can name them by memory. Usually SLPs start with *answering* questions. This makes sense if we are developing receptive language abilities in isolation. But we are here to develop receptive and expressive abilities simultaneously.

Answer "WH" Questions

Whew!!! Take a deep breath, we are back in familiar territory. Now that we know what to answer, we are going to answer the four main questions. However, we are going to answer them in the most robust of ways.

The following three templates are a great place to start. Remember the section on Brain-Based Learning? We want to engage our students with activity such as drawing, writing words, and even creating games. If you are using a storybook that you use frequently, you would benefit from creating your own "WH" question cards for your favorite story.

Instructions:

- Print out the eight-box template. We print it off on four different colored pages. To keep it consistent (and so I don't forget!), I use the first four colors of the rainbow for WHO (red), WHAT (orange), WHEN (yellow), WHERE (green).

- Type or write the questions on one side of the page (e.g. eight WHO questions on the red page) and put the answers on the back.

- BONUS IDEA! Have your 4th and 5th graders make the cards in their therapy sessions for you to use in your younger sessions and keep forever!

"WH" Question Cards / *Tarjetas para preguntas de comprensión*

Fill in cards with "WH" questions about the story. This can also be an activity that the students partake in. Use these decks for games and activities.

Rellene tarjetas con preguntas acerca del cuento. Esto también puede ser una actividad en que los estudiantes participan. Utilice estas cubiertas para los juegos y actividades.

_____	_____
_____	_____
_____	_____
_____	_____

Answering Questions

Use this visual to help children comprehend the meaning of question words. They can write or draw their answers. Laminate this for continued use with dry erase markers.

Contestar preguntas

Utilice esta visual para ayudar a los niños comprender el significado de las palabras de interrogación. Pueden escribir o dibujar sus respuestas. Lamine esto para uso continuo con marcadores de borrado en seco.

Identifying WHO/WHAT/WHEN/WHERE - Examples

This first example in Spanish is from a second-grade student answering "WH" questions with the book *Martha Speaks*.

This second example is a game created for How the Grinch Stole Christmas. The WHERE setting is in the middle and the game pieces are the characters or the WHO.

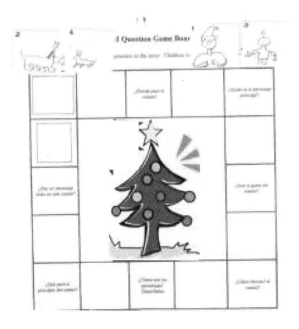

WH Question Game Board

Create game pieces with the characters in the story. Children love to decorate their own game and take it home.

→		Where did the story take place?		Who is the main character?
Is there a bad person in the story?				What did you like about the story?
What happened at the beginning of the story?		What are the characters like? Describe them.		How did the story end?

1	2	3	4

LITERACY-BASED TEMPLATES

Juego de hacer preguntas

Crear piezas del juego con los personajes de la historia. Los niños les encantan decorar su propio juego y llevarlo a casa.

		¿Dónde pasó el cuento?		¿Quién es el personaje principal?
¿Hay un personaje malo en este cuento?				¿Qué te gusta del cuento?
¿Qué pasó al principio del cuento?		¿Cómo son los personajes? Descríbalos.		¿Cómo terminó el cuento?

1	2	3	4

Writing a 4-Part Narrative

For some (most) students, the 16-part narrative is still too big of a leap. We start by creating a story that has a single picture with four parts. It is practice for what's to come. Younger students can draw a picture and you can write what they say, older students don't even need to draw the picture if they are writing at higher level already. Begin by having them attempt to tell the story and write or draw what they think was in it.

- Write WHO-WHAT-WHEN-WHERE on the paper (or copy you doing it)
- Circle WHO-WHAT-WHEN-WHERE with 4 different colors
- Color by Color, correct their work together
- "Let's start with WHO. My WHO is RED."
- "WHO tells us the_____, *that's right the person.*"
- "Look at your picture/sentence, did you include the person?"
- Eventually they can switch papers with their groupmates to correct each other's work and eventually self-correct.

Two important notes:

- Throughout all of these activities, YOU are doing the same thing alongside them. Have a template out for yourself and be drawing, writing, and circling.
- Remember what we said about data collection? They are taking it for you. "STUDENT answered x/4 "WH" questions with a model..."

Here are some examples using *Cactus Soup* and *Chato and His Friends*. They are a little hard to read but we wanted to convey the general idea.

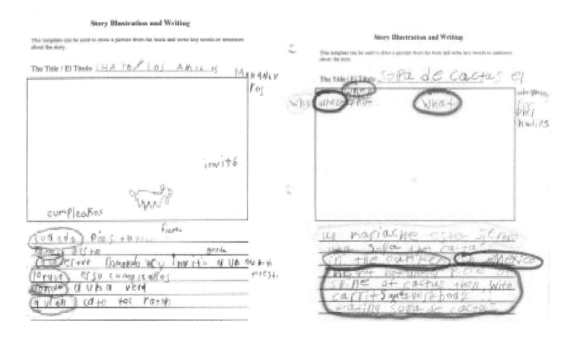

Story Illustration and Writing / *Illustrar y escribir del cuento*

Use this template to draw a picture from the book and write key words or sentences about the story.

Usa esta plantilla para dibujar un dibujo del cuento y escribe palabras claves u oraciones que se tratan del cuento.

The Title/*El Título* :_____

Creating a 16-Part Narrative Story

Hopefully by now, a few things are obvious to you. Can you see how you will be able to stretch your therapy for one book out to several weeks? Can you see why our students are so successful producing complex narrative language. At this point, your students have some mastery over sequencing, using cohesive elements, and creating a four-part story. Not it is time to put it all together and knock your teachers' socks off!

Write the four cohesive elements on the page

We start by writing out the four cohesive elements on the page. This usually begins by them watching you. Within a week, my students know the expectation and write out the four words without asking.

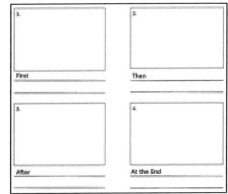

Draw a picture or write a sentence

Most elementary students like to draw but by 3rd grade, some students are impatient and their writing skills take over. It is fine if they only want to write the story. This is the end goal anyway! The template helps them know that they need at least four parts. I had a 4th grade student come to my room complaining about his teachers who made them write paragraphs. I explained that a paragraph has 3-5 sentences and that he had written about 20 paragraphs in my class this year so far. It was just that our four sentences were spread around the page. He asked me if I kept all of his homework so that he could show his teacher so that he didn't have to write anymore!

Write the four question words on the page

Again, the students typically follow me first but soon do it by memory.

Circle the question words in four different colors

If you stick with the rainbow order, it is easier to remember in the long run. WHO (red), WHAT (orange), WHEN (yellow), and WHERE (green). Consistency is important for our students.

Grade work collectively and then individually

I usually work through the whole group for each individual question. If a student is missing a component, pause for second and add the part to their picture or sentence. No punishment or celebration, they just know they are done when they have 16 parts. Celebrating is for *more* than 16 circles.

I have students who can independently create 10-12 part stories right off the bat, and then self-correct and bring it up to 16 parts. Better yet, they know 1) if they are missing a part and 2) exactly what they are missing when they ask for help. Here are some examples from students at different levels for both fiction and non-fiction stories.

Non-fiction Teacher Example about Thanksgiving

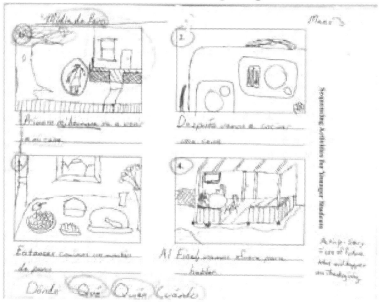

Second-Grade Female with Limited Expressive and Receptive Abilities

Second-Grade Male with Limited Expressive and Receptive Abilities

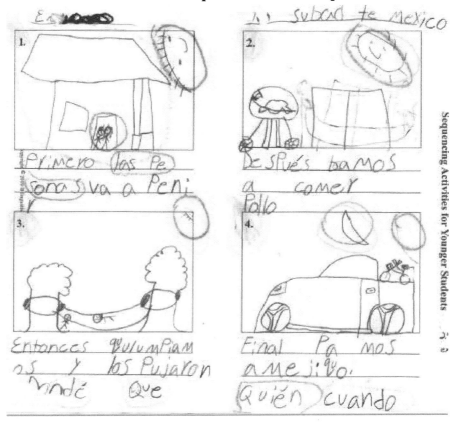

First-Grade Male with Expressive Language and Articulation Goals

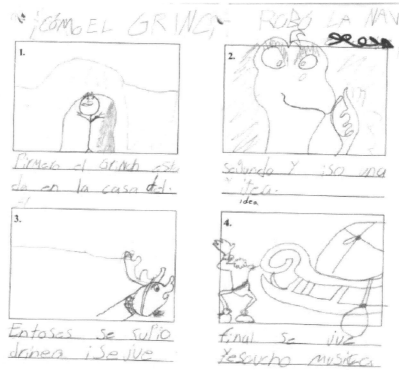

5-year-old Working on Expressive Language and Social Skills

Khoa is working on the telling of Jerry Pinkey's *The Lion & The Mouse*, a wordless picture book about the friendship between a lion and a mouse.

Language/Social Skills Group with 3rd, 4th, 5th graders: collaborative story.

Plot Summary: It was Friday the 13th, and two boys, Thomas and Nicky, plan to go to Target. As they walked there, they accidently walked under a ladder. First, a car drove by and splashed them with a puddle of dog urine. Then, they were struck by lightning. Last, a hurricane came and picked them up. They spun and spun. Finally, they landed on top of the Target. Thomas says, "We are at Target!" Nicky says, "How are we going to get down?!" The end.

Fifth Grader (in Life Skills Classroom): Receptive and Expressive Language and Social Skills Goals

Using Poetry with a portion of Edgar Allan Poe's *Annabel Lee*

It was many and many a year ago,

  In a kingdom by the sea,

That a maiden there lived whom you may know

  By the name of Annabel Lee;

And this maiden she lived with no other thought

  Than to love and be loved by me.

I was a child and she was a child,

  In this kingdom by the sea,

But we loved with a love that was more than love—

  I and my Annabel Lee—

With a love that the wingèd seraphs of Heaven

  Coveted her and me.

And this was the reason that, long ago,

  In this kingdom by the sea,

A wind blew out of a cloud, chilling

  My beautiful Annabel Lee;

So that her highborn kinsmen came

  And bore her away from me,

To shut her up in a sepulchre

  In this kingdom by the sea.

LITERACY-BASED TEMPLATES

16-Part Narrative Story Template

2.

4.

1.

3.

Story Recall, Sequencing, and Narrative Components
Recontar un cuento, la secuencia, y las partes narrativas

Title/*Título*: _____

Name/*Nombre*: _____

	Characters / *Las personajes*
	Setting When / *Escenario- Cuándo*
	Setting- Where / *Escenario- Dónde*
	Probem / *El problema*
	Solution / *La solución*
	Events / *Los eventos*
	Feelings / *Los sentimientos*
	Resolution / *La Resolución*

LITERACY-BASED TEMPLATES

Sequencing Activities for Older Students Template

Name / Nombre:_____ Date /Fecha:_____

Title / El título:

Place / El lugar:

Characters / Los personajes:

What happened at the beginning of the story? / ¿Qué pasó al principio del cuento?

What happened in the middle of the story? / ¿Qué pasó en el medio del cuento?

What happened at the end of the story? / ¿Qué pasó al final del cuento?

Problem / El problema:

Solution / La solución:

Sentence Expansion Activities: Describing by Category, Attribute, and Function Exercise

Instructions:

1. Lay out pictures of story vocabulary or create a list of words from the story
2. Use this structure to expand sentences by describing an item by its category and attributes

This graph provides a structure for a student to say "A _____ is a _____ that_____." The end goal is to have the student produce a rich utterance without the support of the chart.

Name	Category	Attribute	Function
Ex. A ball	is a toy	that is round	that you can throw
_____	is	that is	that you

Expandir las oraciones: Describir palabras por su categoría, atributos, y función

Instrucciones:

1. Coloque fotos de vocabulario o crear una lista de palabras a partir de un cuento.
2. Utilice esta estructura para expandir oraciones describiendo un elemento por su categoría y atributos.

Esta gráfica proporciona una estructura para un estudiante que decir "Un _____ es un tipo de _____ que es_____ y que se usa para _____." El objetivo final: que el estudiante produzca una oración larga sin el apoyo de la gráfica.

el uso	atributo	grupo	El nombre
y se puede tirar	*que es redonda*	*es un juguete*	*La pelota*
que se puede	que es	es	

Comparing and Contrasting Two Stories

Use each story you read as an opportunity for the student to create their own story. Use the storybook's structure to invent and tell a story.

For example, *"The Three Little Pigs"* can become " The Three Little Fish" who move into a bed of reeds, a reef, and a cave to avoid the big bad shark.

	Setting	Secondary Characters	Main Character	Title
Your Story				

Comparar y contrastar dos cuentos

Utilice cada historia que lea como una oportunidad para que el estudiante cree su propia historia. Utilice la estructura del libro de cuentos para inventar y contar una historia.

Por ejemplo, "*Los tres cerditos*" pueden convertirse en "*Los tres pequeños peces*" que se mueven en una cama de cañas, un arrecife, y una cueva para evitar el tiburón grande y malo.

La escena		
Los personajes secundarios		
El personaje principal		
El título	*Tu cuento*	

Answering Questions Cube Printout

Use this die during games or question-asking activities. Students can cut and color the die themselves.

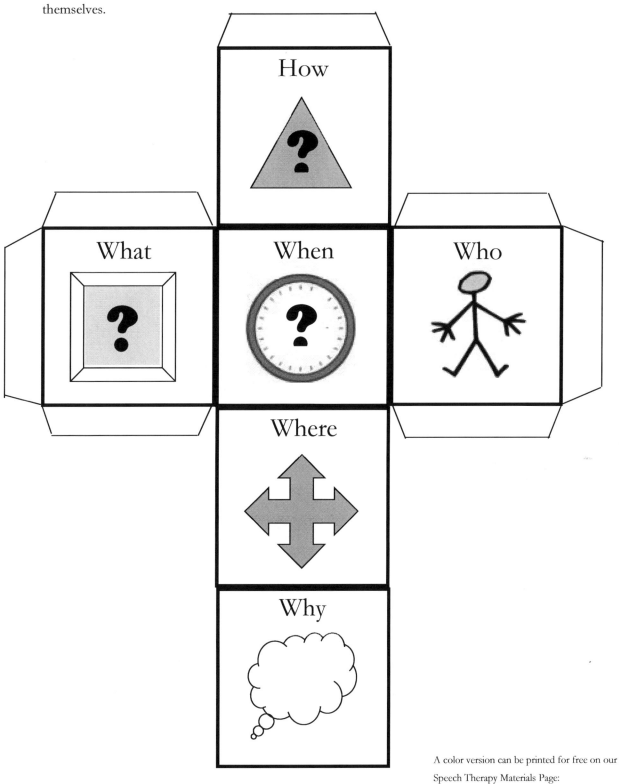

A color version can be printed for free on our Speech Therapy Materials Page:

https://bilinguistics.com/speech-therapy-materials/

Preguntas de Respuesta Impresión de Cubo

Utilice este dado durante los juegos o preguntas que hacen las actividades. Los estudiantes pueden cortar y colorear el dado ellos mismos.

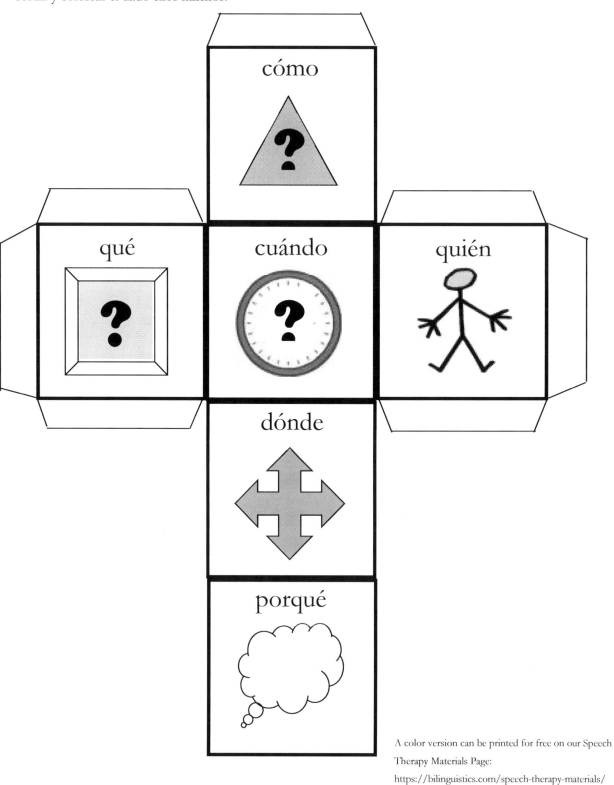

Folding Story-Parts Maker Instructions

This folding story-parts maker allows a student to separate the story into beginning, middle, and end, draw a picture of the events, and write a sentence about the story. For older students, we also have them identify WHO-WHAT-WHERE for each portions of the story.

Instructions: Cut the template out and cut in between all of the first squares. Fold them over and write BEGINNING, MIDDLE, END, or whatever you want to include inside.

Have the students draw a picture on the inside and/or write about the story based on their level.

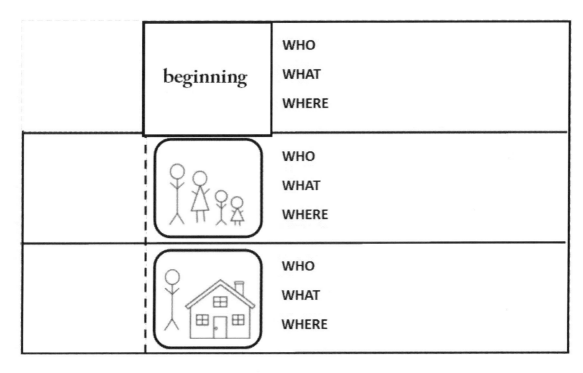

Folding Story-Parts Maker

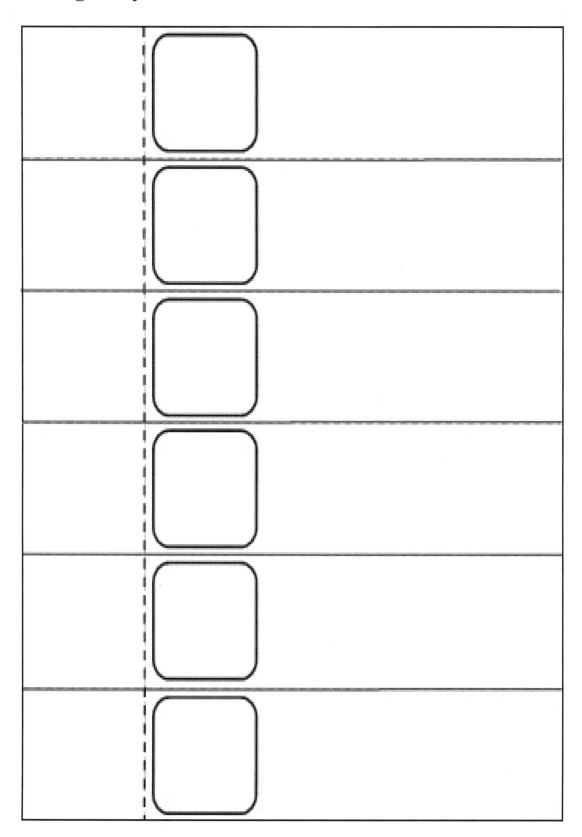

Character Information Pop-Up

Instructions: Have your students draw a character and fill in information about what the character might think or say. Cut out all three pieces. Fold the largest piece into a right angle. Bend the tabs of the small rectangle back and glue tabs to the designated spot on the sheet. Glue the person against small rectangle front. The character will be standing on the base with the thought bubbles behind him.

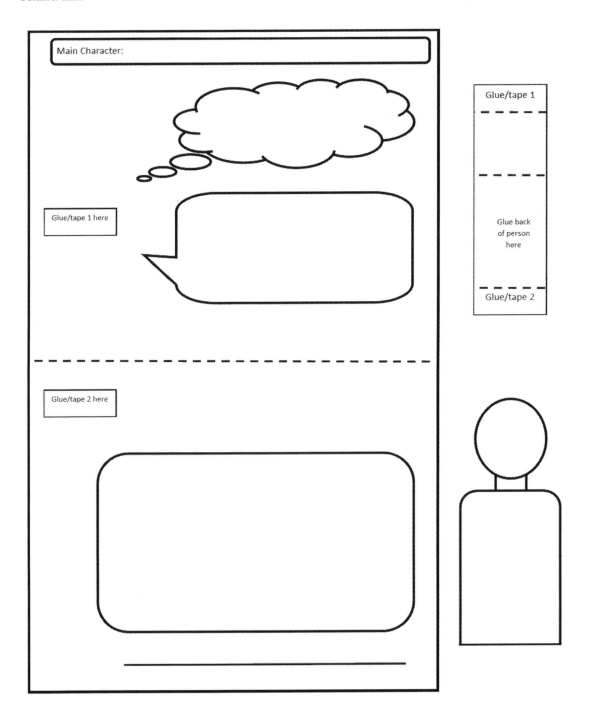

Think - Pair - Share

Test acquired knowledge by having group members pair up and share what they know about aspects of their story. Combine all of their details here together on one template.

Book Title:	
Partner 1 Shared:	**Partner 2 Shared:**

Categorization Graphic Organizer

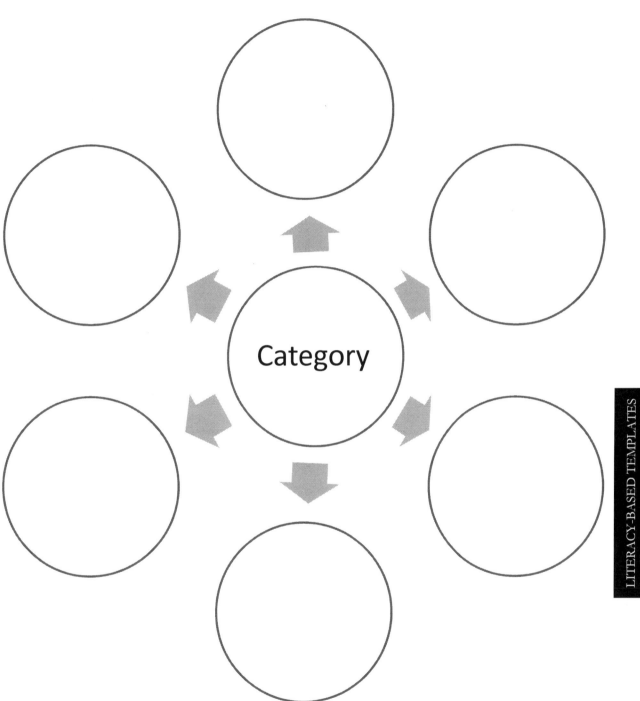

Function Attribute Category Therapy (FACT) Map for Sentence Expansion

Use the template to have a child move downward to discuss the category and attributes of an object in order to expand their sentence. For example: Place the COW in the name block and begin moving down: "A cow (name) is an animal (category) that lives on a **farm**/jungle/ocean, says **moo**/oink/woof, or flies/**walks**/swims (attribute/function).

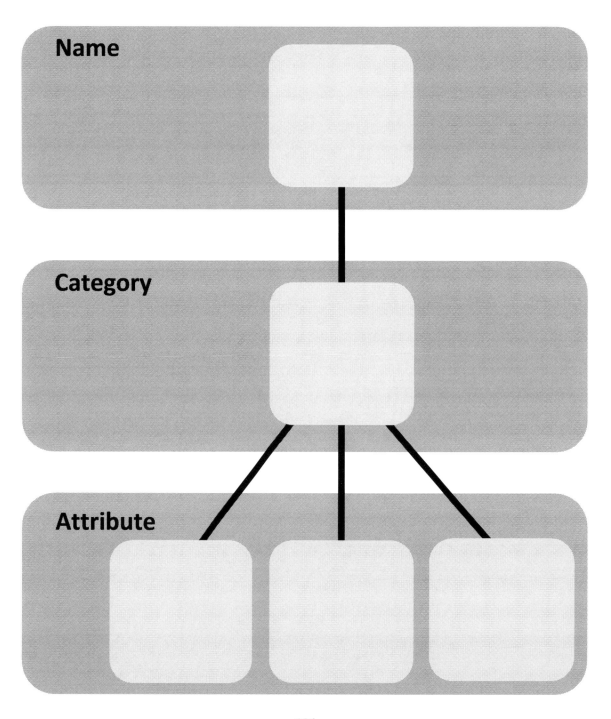

Name

Category

Attribute

Mapa de función, atributo, y categoría para expandir las oraciones

Utilice la plantilla para pedir al estudiante que se mueva hacia abajo para hablar de la categoría y los atributos de un para expandir sus oraciones. Por ejemplo: Coloca la vaca en el cuadro de nombre y comenzar a moverse hacia abajo: "Una vaca (nombre) es un animal (categoría) que vive en una **granja**/selva/océano, dice **mu**/oink/guau, o vuela/**camina**/nada (atributo/función).

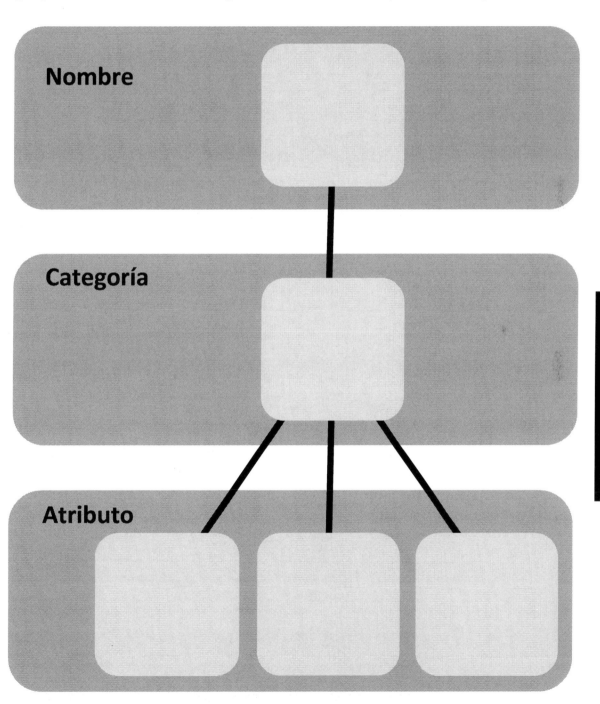

Nombre

Categoría

Atributo

Puppet Sticks

Create puppets by drawing or copying the characters from the story so that the story can be told from the characters' point of view and from their actions.

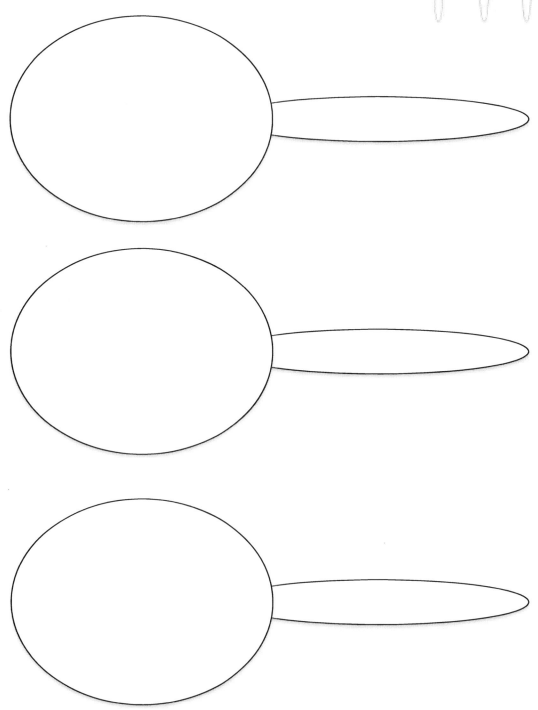

Accordion Books

A fun take-home activity to use with cumulative stories is an accordion book that opens up to more and pictures with each turn of the page. The student can glue each picture on the strip and by the end, they have a completely sequenced story. Here is an example from *The Gigantic Turnip* and all the help that the farmer gets to try to pull the turnip out of the ground.

How to Make an Accordion Book.

- Take an 8.5×11 piece of paper and cut it in half length-wise. If it is a long story, tape the two short ends of each half sheet together, so you have one very long strip of paper.
- Fold the paper in half, width wise. Open the paper and fold the ends of the paper, in equal sized sections, towards the midline. If you are using an 11 inch long piece of paper, you will have a total of 6 equal sized sections.
- On one side of the paper you will put pictures from the story in REVERSE order, from RIGHT to LEFT:

1. Picture of the problem, or initiating event
2. First attempt at the solution/First event in the cumulative sequence
3. Second attempt at the solution/Second event in the cumulative sequence
4. Third attempt at the solution/Third event in the cumulative sequence
5. Fourth attempt at the solution/Fourth event in the cumulative sequence
6. Picture of the resolution of the story and/or the words "The End!"
7. On the other side of the paper, put the title of the story on the second section (when going from LEFT to RIGHT). The rest of the sections on this side will be left blank.
8. Now, turn the paper back over and fold in each section over the one in front of it, folding from LEFT to RIGHT. The title page should appear on the front after the last fold.
9. To read your accordion book, open the title page first and you'll see the initiating event. Keep unfolding your book to show the sequential attempts at the solution. The previous attempts will still be showing, so you can repeat each attempt at solving the problem (much like what is done in these cumulative stories).

Accordion Books Template

Venn Diagram / *Diagrama de Venn*

Have the child describe two different items (broccoli/celery) or two different categories (fruit/vegetables). Discuss features that are alike and different.

Haga que el estudiante describa dos cosas diferentes (broccoli/apio) o dos categorías diferentes (fruta/verduras). Hable de cómo se parecen y cómo son diferentes.

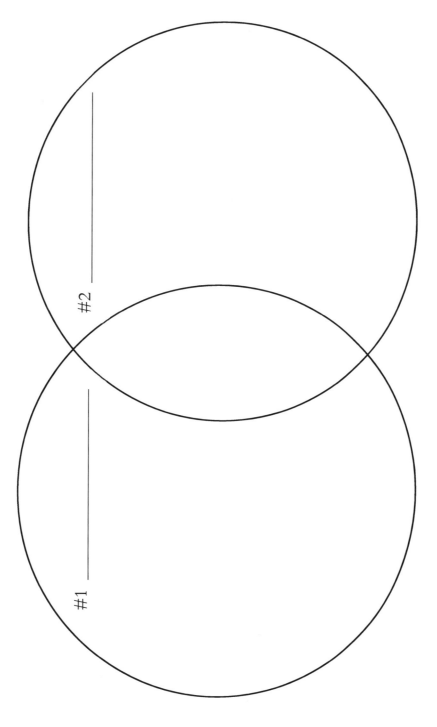

LITERACY-BASED TEMPLATES

Articulation – Words from books chart

Go through the book and write down high frequency words that match articulation targets.

Sound	Initial	Medial	Final	Clusters
/b/				
/p/				
/m/				
/w/				
/d/				

Articulation – Words from books chart

Go through the book and write down high frequency words that match articulation targets.

Sound	Initial	Medial	Final	Clusters
/t/				
/n/				
/l/				
/g/				
/k/				

Articulation – Words from books chart

Go through the book and write down high frequency words that match articulation targets.

Sound	Initial	Medial	Final	Clusters
/f/				
/s/				
/r/				
/ch/				
/dg/				

Word Lists by Sound and Homework

Use these following graphs to group words from the story by their sounds. These graphs can also serve as homework assignments. Four to five of these sheets should be printed out per book to include all sounds addressed in intervention or in the classroom.

Practicing the words from the story: _____

Sound		Sound	Sound	
	*			

Parents, please practice these words with your child and put a check next to each word as they practice the sound.

Listas de palabras por el sonido y la tarea

Utilice estos gráficos siguientes para agrupar las palabras del cuento por sus sonidos. Estos gráficos también pueden servir como tareas. De cuatro a cinco de estas hojas deben imprimirse por libro para incluir todos los sonidos en que están trabajando en la terapia o en el aula.

Practicando las palabras del cuento:_____

Sonido	*	Sonido		Sonido	

Favor de practicar todas las palabras 5-10 veces con su hijo(a). Ponga una palomita al lado de cada palabra después de practicarla.

3-year-old with speech sound disorder working on final /t/ and final /d/

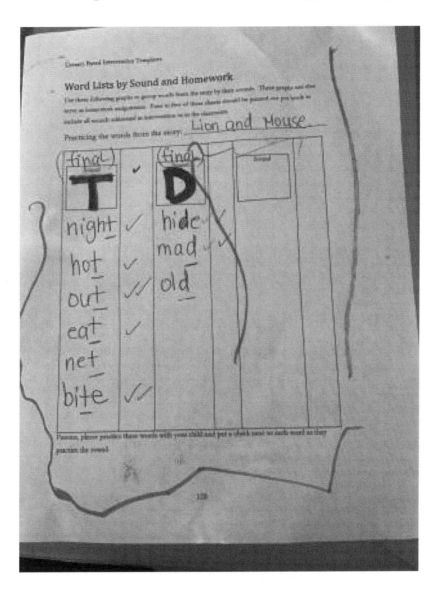

Blank Sound Chart

Sound charts similar to this can easily be created for any book to track a student's sound productions.

Example: This articulation chart was created for: *The Gigantic Turnip* by Aleksei Tolstoy and Niamh Sharkey

WORD	B	P	M	D	T	N	K	G	L	R	W	TH	BLEND
Turnip		▓			▓	▓				▓			
Cow							▓				▓		
Grow								▓		▓	▓		▓

WORD	B	P	M	D	T	N	K	G	L	R	W	TH	BLEND
Total													

Tabla de sonidos

Los gráficos de sonido cono este ejemplo se pueden crear fácilmente para cualquier libro para rastrear las producciones de sonido de un estudiante.

Ejemplo: Esta tabla de articulación fue creada para: *El Nabo Gigante* por Aleksei Tolstoy y Niamh Sharkey.

Palabra	K	G	S	D	N	L	T	R	RR	Y	Grupos de sonidos
Raton					▓		▓		▓		
Cayó	▓									▓	
Cerditos			▓	▓			▓				

Palabra	K	G	S	D	N	L	T	R	RR	Y	agrupado
Total											

6. Creating Incredible Games that Match Story Content

Speech Therapists Just Play Games!

Have you heard this? Maybe it was uttered by another educator as they passed through our therapy room. Maybe it was shared by a parent who was watching our session in the home or clinic. The onlookers were aware of the fun being had but innocently unaware of the focus of the activity. The truth is that there are a lot of things that we do that could be characterized as "having fun." In these cases, we can easily justify our activities with explanations of the goals that we are focusing on and the desired outcome.

Games and play create a perfect storm of some of the highest levels of engagement, open minds, motivation to remember through competition, and just plain fun. What is lacking, and what this section promises to share research information showing that structured game-playing is an effective way to solidify your speech and language gains. Justifying what we do is only a tiny part of it. Storybooks generally fall into eight narrative categories that make their outcome "predictable" in certain ways. By learning about these eight types of predictable books, we can generate board games that match the narrative structure. If a child learns (or makes) a game, a child learns the structure. Boom! Try to pull that off with other therapeutic techniques!

Predictable books make use of rhyme, repetition of words, phrases, sentences and refrains, and such patterns as cumulative structure, repeated scenes, familiar cultural sequences, interlocking structure and turn-around plots. These stories invite children to make predictions or guesses about words, phrases, sentences, events and characters that could come next in the story.

- Mary Jett Simpson, in Reading Resource Book

Predictable books allow early readers to predict what the sentences are going to say, thereby increasing enjoyment and helping to build vocabulary and memory skills.

-www.educationoasis.com

What are Predictable Books?

Predictable books have structured patterns so that a reader can anticipate upcoming story events. They employ repetitive lines, plots, refrains, rhythm, or phrases. The books for younger children contain visuals to help tell the story.

Why Are Predictable Books Important?

If the idea of predictable books is new to you, you are in for a real treat. One of the best ways to increase a child's participation (without relying on his or her ability to demonstrate reading fluency and comprehension), is to select a book that has repetition and predictability. Predictable books have been a hot topic with educators, librarians, and literacy coaches for many years, and for good reasons. **Here are just a few of the benefits of predictable books:**

High level of participation:
The familiarity that the stories generate, the rhyming, and the repetitive nature encourages children to take an active role in the story-telling rather than simply listening.

Pre-reading skills
Predictable books introduce the most common grammatical constructs and also compare and contrast sounds with rhyming words. The quick pace of several of the book types teaches how to progress through a book from top to bottom, left to right, and page to page.

Natural inflection
The natural inflection that we use in daily conversation is conveyed through the story-telling of predictable books. Because of the high level of repetition, children have an opportunity to practice and play with the nuances of language.

Narrative structure
Predictable books introduce the most common and basic story structures which are the foundation for understanding plot and story-writing in the older grades.

Utterance expansion
The repetitive nature of predictable books and the rhyme schemes enable a child to produce longer utterances than they would normally use. This is extremely important for children with expressive language impairments and phonological delays who typically produce communication that is short, relative to their age. Predictable books create a framework to explore and practice longer words and utterances.

Types of Predictable Books

There are eight different types of predictable books. We can use these eight groups to categorize the books we read and get a better understanding of what each book has to offer. These predictable categories also enable us to better define *WHY* our favorite books for speech therapy are successful, thus helping identify other book titles for future sessions.

1. **Chain or Circular Story:** The story's ending leads back to the beginning. Example: *Where the Wild Things Are*

2. **Cumulative Story:** The story builds on a pattern. It starts with one person, place, thing, or event. Each time a new person, place, thing, or event is shown, all the previous ones are repeated. Example: *There was an Old Lady Who Swallowed a Fly*

3. **Familiar Sequence Story:** A common, recognizable theme such as the days of the week, the months, etc. Example: *Today is Monday*

4. **Pattern Story:** The scenes or episodes are repeated with a variation. Example: *Froggy Gets Dressed*

5. **Question and Answer Book:** A question is repeated throughout the story. Example: *Brown Bear, Brown Bear*

6. **Repetition of Phrase Book:** A phrase or sentence is repeated. Example: *Goodnight Moon*

7. **Rhyme Book:** A rhyme, refrain, or rhythm is repeated throughout the story. Example: *Chicka Chicka Boom Boom*

8. **Song Book:** Familiar songs with repeated phrases, sentences, rhymes, or refrains. Example: *Five Little Monkeys*

Note that predictable themes are easier to identify with books written for younger children. We often see more overlap of characteristics in different types of predictable books in stories written for older children, as they contain more story elements. Let's talk about each type of predictable book in-depth and the natural way these books lend themselves to being taught through games. Some storybooks are predictable in several ways. For example, *Brown Bear, Brown Bear, What Do You See?* both rhymes and follows a pattern. We have grouped the following books based on how we have used them successfully in therapy.

How to Leverage Predictable Narratives and Gaming to Make Communication Gains

Now that we have learned a bit about predictable books, let's talk about types of games and the way we play. Yes, games come in boxes and line our shelves but we need to reach back into the memories of our childhood and reintroduce ourselves to the games we played in and around our neighborhood. We also need to open our minds forward and think of all the possibilities that apps and websites could afford us. If it matches the narrative structure of a book, it is "fair game."

Types of Games:

Board Games

We all have our favorites. Think of yours. No, **truly think of yours.** *Monopoly* is a cumulative story where you are a realty investor and you travel around accumulating wealth. So is *Sorry!* Winners accumulate. *Trivial Pursuit* is both a cumulative and question and answer game.

Scavenger Hunt – Searches

Tag, 7-Steps Around the House, Marco Polo, Oh Captain My Captain, Capture the Flag. If there was a reason I was getting grounded in the summer when I was young, chances are I didn't come home when I was in the middle of a scavenger hunt -search game. Leaving the game would have been against the law, basically, or so I told my mom. There are books like *Going on a Bear Hunt* or *Are You My Mother?* which can be reenacted with 10 stick-figure drawings and a trip around your school yard.

Imitation and Follow Directions Games

I was teaching my students Go-Go-Stop when a passerby asked, "Are you from up north?" When I said I was, she said: "It's called Red-Light Green-Light down here." My student immediately knew what to do. Statues and Simon Says are both imitation games. You can get your students out of their chairs with books like *Mr. Brown Can Moo, Can You?* or *From Head to Toe* and move your way through the plot.

Patty-Cake Type Games

I don't know if this is an actual genre of games, perhaps I made it up. But that is kind of the point of clapping/rhythm games, you make them up. Beat on the table, clap, work with partners, or make up a pattern by taping on your body. Middle schoolers often know hand-clap series that go with jump-ropeish (second made up word!) songs that boggle the mind. There is something about creating the beats that also generates loud responses as students really get into it and compete with the noise.

This, folks, is also brain-based learning and engagement. Check out the book: Anna Banana: 101 Jump Rope Rhymes.

Bingo

Bingo is in a class of its own and is the black pepper of games. You can throw it into anything you are cooking up. Reading *Bear on a Bike*? Transportation Bingo. *Brown Bear*? Animal Bingo. *Hungry Caterpillar*? Food Bingo. If you do not know where to start or are short on time, start with Bingo.

Games are Stories – Stories are Games

My goal in this section is to blur the lines between games and stories. They are the same! Narratives are powerful at linking together tons of details. Think about all the kids participating in extremely complex online universes. There would be no way to remember all the places, characters, powers, etc. without the story and its narrative glue. Now, we are going to reverse engineer the process.

We are going to turn the paradigm on its head and use the *game* to teach the *narrative*.

Your job is to:

1. Choose a book you love

2. Identify what narrative structure it has

3. Map the story onto a game that has the same structure

(or keep reading)

How to Make Games

The bright people that make games don't think like speech-language pathologists. This means we have to make games from scratch. Here are some powerful time- and effort-saving tips:

- Always use manila folders for physical games. They are easy to carry and to store. They can be laminated. The kids can make their own.
- Make it once for your favorite book and create a box/folder/binder of everything related to that book. We have a library of binders in our office. Each binder has the blank templates from the previous section, the books in a pouch, everything related to the book and a game or two. We have a checkout system where we have a list of all of our literacy-kits and everyone has a clothespin with their name on it to mark what kit they have out.
- Have your students make their own games! Now that's learning.
- Have your older students make *your* games at the end of each book. They LOVE it and you have incredible keepsakes.

Chain or Circular Stories

A Circular or Chain Story is a story that begins and ends in the same place, such as *Where the Wild Things Are* or *If You Give a Mouse a Cookie.*

library → park → store → home → school → library (circular diagram)

Chain or circular stories are great for therapy because:

- Many have a great macrostructure of beginning, middle, and end, which helps us teach sequencing.

- They contain the "typical" macrostructure elements such as characters, setting (time and place), problem, solution, initiating event, character intentions and desires, and moral.

- The end of the story comes around full circle, which gives a great opportunity to work on story organization/structure, and making predictions on how a story might end.

- Many have some sort of cause and effect or problem and solution that can be discussed.

- They can be adapted across age/grade levels to work at the cognitive level of the student(s).

How to use Chain or Circular or Stories in Speech Therapy

Here is one of our favorite chain or circular stories and examples of how we use it in therapy to target a variety of goals:

Where the Wild Things Are/Donde Viven Los Monstruos

by Maurice Sendak.

Goal:	English	Spanish
Articulation	/r/, /s/ blends, /th/	/r/ blends, /s/ blends, Final consonants (/s/ and /n/)
Syntax	Past tense sentence structure (ex. Wore, grew, sailed, etc.)	Past tense structure (e.g. puso, dijo, nació, creció, etc.)- Noun/verb agreement- singular vs. plural

Conjunctions	Compound sentences conjoined with "and" and "so."	Compound sentences conjoined with "y."
Semantics *Strategies to learn new vocabulary*	Body parts- eyes, teeth, claws and other "Wild Thing" body parts	Body parts- ojos, dientes, garras, etc.
	New terms-mischief, gnashed, rumpus	New terms- travesura, rugidos, crujieron, afilados, centellaeantes
Wh- questions	What, who, where, when, why	Qué, quién, dónde, cuándo, por qué
Macrostructure- story elements, structure, organization of a narrative	Sequencing, story elements (characters, setting (time and place), problem, solution, initiating event, character intentions and desires, moral)	

Chain or Circular Story Games

Circular stories are actually the easiest to create because they truly resemble board games. In *Where the Wild Things Are*, Max gets in trouble and is sent to his room, crosses the ocean and goes to where the wild things are, crosses the ocean back, and returns to his room.

Chain or Circular Stories for Speech Therapy

	Title	Description of Story
	**A Chair for My Mother** **Un sillón para mi mamá**	Plot: A family must work together with their community to rebuild their home after a fire. Why we like it: Plot, culture, great opportunities for visualizing and describing.
	**Knufflebunny** **El conejito Knuffle**	Plot: On an errand to the laundromat, Trixie loses her beloved stuffed bunny and must figure out where he's gone. Why we like it: Students identify with Trixie's struggle to express herself.
	**The Snowy Day** **Un dia de nieve**	Plot: A little boy plays outside in the snow and then goes home to tell his mom all about it. Why we like it: Lots of opportunities for predicting, sequencing, and talking about the winter season.
	**If You Give a Mouse a Cookie** **Si le das una galletita a un ratón**	Plot: When a mouse invites himself into the house and is given a cookie, a number of entertaining consequences ensue. Why we like it: It's a good way to introduce the concept of cause and effect and can be used for sequencing and predicting.
	**If You Give a Moose a Muffin** **Si le das un panecillo a un alce**	Plot: A surprise guest invites himself in and again takes advantage of a boy's hospitality in an entertaining way. Why we like it: Similar to its predecessor, it's also great for sequencing and making predictions, working on sentence building and vocabulary.

MAKING THERAPY GAMES

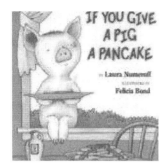

If You Give a Pig a Pancake

Si le das un panqueque a una cerdita

Plot: Following the similar structure of other circular stories by this author, a pig is given a pancake leading to a chain of consequences. Comical exploration concept, "If you give an inch, they'll take a mile."

Why we like it: Similar to its predecessors, but with a female protagonist, it's great for teaching cause and effect, predictions, and sequencing in a humorous light.

Where the Wild Things Are

Donde viven los monstruos

Plot: A little boy imagines himself traveling to a far away place, where he makes unlikely friends and learns to appreciate what he has at home when he returns.

Why we like it: Great story for inspiring children's imaginations, wonderful book for working on consonant clusters.

Why Mosquitos Buzz in People's Ears

Porque zumban los mosquitos en los oidos

Plot: A mosquito tells a lie to an iguana and sets off a series of events. It is a 'fable-like' story.

Why we like it: It teaches the value of telling the truth, and is great for visualizing, describing, and sequencing. It provides a context to learn about different animals, cause and effect, and has beautiful illustrations.

The Rainbow Fish

El pez arco iris

Plot: A proud fish learns a lesson about valuing inner beauty and friendship.

Why we like it: Lovely illustrations, fairly predictable story that is good for vocabulary building, semantic mapping, and teaching predictions and inferencing. Great story for working on social/pragmatic skills (friendship building/initiating play).

Cumulative Stories

A cumulative story is a story that builds on a pattern. It starts with one person, place, thing, or event. Each time a new person, place, thing, or event is shown, all the previous ones are repeated, such as, *There Was an Old Lady Who Swallowed a Fly.*

Cumulative stories are great for therapy because:

- There is LOTS of repetition, repetition, repetition (can you say, "Increased number of productions?!"). We love this for teaching a new sentence structure and for articulation practice.

- The macrostructure tends to be a problem/solution type of structure. Each event reinforces the initiating problem of the story and a new attempt at solving it. It helps children to think outside of the box of different solutions to the same problem.

- Many contain the "typical" macrostructure elements such as characters, setting (time and place), problem, solution, initiating event, character intentions and desires, and moral.

- The end of the story is distinctly different from all the previous, reduplicated events. This gives the end of the story an OOMPH that can be used to teach the concept of wrapping up a story with a strong ending.

- There are many opportunities for predicting what might happen next. Many times, the sequential events (and attempts to solve the problem) are the same, so the child can pick up on that pattern. The final, different event makes predicting even more fun and shows that there can be numerous ways to make a prediction.

- They can be adapted across age/grade levels, to work at the cognitive level of the student(s).

How to use Cumulative Stories in Speech Therapy

As an example, here is one of our favorite cumulative stories, and how we like to use it in therapy to target a variety of goals:

The Giant Turnip/El Nabo Gigante

by Aleksei Tolstoy and Niamh Sharkey

Goal:	English	Spanish
Articulation	Final consonants, vocalic /r/	/s/, /n/, /l/, /k/, multisyllabic words
Syntax	Past tense sentence structure (ex. planted, rained, pulled, etc..)	-Past tense structure (e.g. sembraron, creció, halaron, etc.)- Noun/verb agreement- singular vs. plural
Conjunctions	Compound sentences conjoined with "but," "still," "so"	Compound sentences conjoined with "pero," "aún," "así que"
Semantics	Vegetable and planting vocabulary, descriptive terms (colors, size), seasons	
Wh- questions	What, who, where, when, why	Qué, quién, dónde, cuándo, por qué
Macrostructure- story elements, structure, organization of a narrative	Sequencing- planting Story elements (characters, setting (time and place), problem, solution, initiating event, character intentions and desires, moral)	

Cumulative Story Games

Cumulative stories do just that, they accumulate. A character moves through a story and collects objects, eat things, or gathers friends to support an outcome. In the *Gigantic Turnip*, a farmer cannot pull a turnip out of the ground. He slowly gathers his wife, one cow, two pigs, three black cats… to all work together. We made a board game of the characters designed around Trivial Pursuit. A

child collects all the characters on his card and then races to the center to get the last character, the mouse. The winner gets the turnip soup. Here is what the board game looks like when it is all set up:

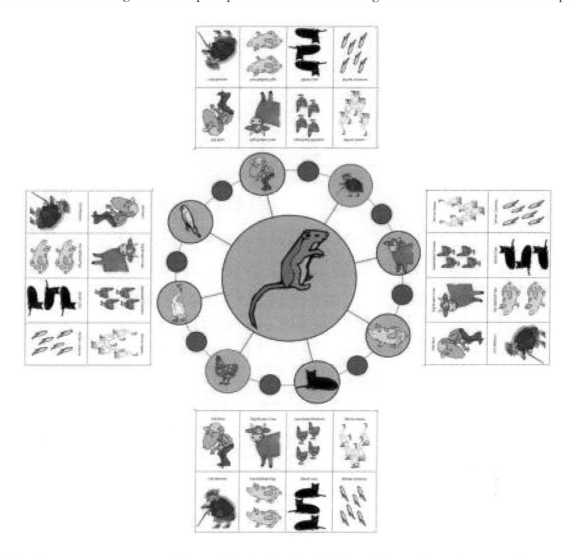

Here is a very common cumulative activity for *Go Away Big Green Monster*. Create four sets of monsters and assemble and unassemble the monster as you yell for him to go away. Kids love this!

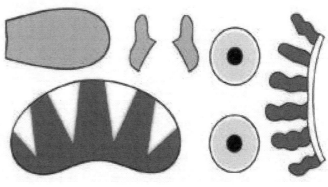

MAKING THERAPY GAMES

Cumulative Stories for Speech Therapy

	Title	Description of Story
	**The Gingerbread Man** **El hombre de pan de jengibre**	A lovely old couple make a child out of gingerbread. He comes to life and escapes them. Animals chase him, trying to eat him. He outsmarts everyone except the fox. Why we like it: Kids will enjoy seeing how the gingerbread man outsmarts the fox, and chant along to the rhythm of the story. Great story for working on action words, describing, sentence building, and /r/ in English and Spanish (along with /rr/ in 'corre').
	**The Gigantic Turnip** **El nabo gigante**	Plot: A farmer and his wife find a giant turnip in their garden that requires cooperation from all the animals on the farm to unroot. Why we like it: Great story for working on wh- questions, /r/ clusters (Spanish), seasons and vegetable/planting vocabulary. It also teaches the value of teamwork.
	**Go Away Big Green Monster** **Fuera de aqui, monstruo verde!**	Plot: While turning the pages of this die-cut book, a big green monster grows then disappears. Why we like it: On each page a new body part is introduced and described. This also a good book for /r/ in English and Spanish. It is best used for ages 3-5 years.
	**There Was an Old Lady Who Swallowed a Fly**	Plot: This is a well-known story of an old lady who swallows one animal after another to catch the preceding one. Why we like it: Children enjoy guessing what the old lady will need to swallow next to catch each animal, and the die-cut illustrations make this fun. This is a good story for targeting animal vocabulary, colors, sequencing, and /s/ and /l/ clusters (English) and /r/ clusters (Spanish).

162

The Little Old Lady Who Wasn't Afraid of Anything

La viejecita quien no tenia miedo de nada

Plot: The story of a little old lady who never gets scared, until one night while walking through the woods she is followed by haunted clothes that form the parts of a scarecrow.

Why we like it: The story has a definitive rhythm, and kids will be chanting along with you during the "chorus" of the story. This is great for working on /s/ and /r/ clusters in Spanish, plurals in both Spanish and English, along with clothing and Halloween vocabulary.

The Cazuela the Farm Maiden Stirred

Plot: The story of how a farm maiden and the farm animals work together to make the rice pudding for the fiesta.

Why we like it: Similarly structured to "The House that Jack Built," this story is good for sequencing, teaching animal names/categories, and has beautiful illustrations for describing. The story is told in English with Spanish words incorporated, so may be best for children who have at least some English, or could also be translated.

Stuck

Atrapados

Plot: When a little boy tries to rescue his kite from a tree, he throws item upon item trying to get it down, only resulting in everything getting stuck!

Why we like it: Whimsical and amusing, kids will laugh out loud. Great for teaching predictions, sequencing, /r/ clusters in English, and teaching expectations.

The Rooster Who Went to His Uncle's Wedding

El gallo que fue a la boda de su tío

Plot: A cumulative Cuban folktale about a rooster who is trying to get clean on the way to his uncle's wedding and encounters humorous setbacks.

Why we like it: This story is appropriate for children aged 5-7 and can easily be used to teach animals, compare and contrast, teach 'if'...'then' and consequences of actions in a light and fun way.

MAKING THERAPY GAMES

Familiar Sequence Stories

Familiar sequence stories are stories that are organized by a recognizable theme such as days of the week, months of the year, numbers, etc. Such as: *Today is Monday.*

Familiar sequence stories are great for therapy because:

- They use sequences that most children have been exposed to, which helps comprehension of the story by tying story events to prior knowledge.
- They provide a context for working on functional vocabulary skills if the child has not yet learned those sequences (such as days of the week)..
- You can easily include the scaffolding strategy of cloze procedure (the therapist begins the phrase and the child fills in the gap. Example: Therapist, " Monday, Tuesday, Wednesday…." Child, "Thursday").
- The rote and automatic production of many of these sequences is great for individuals with fluency disorders and word retrieval difficulties.
- Familiar sequences provide many carryover opportunities far beyond the speech therapy room, into daily life and the classroom.
- They include core vocabulary words to practice both language and articulation.

How to use Familiar Sequence Stories in Speech Therapy

Here is one of our favorite familiar sequence stories and examples of how we use it in therapy to target a variety of goals:

The Hungry Caterpillar/La oruga muy hambrienta

by Eric Carle

Goal:	English	Spanish
Articulation	/s/, /k/, /d/, final consonants	/s/, /k/ and /g/, /r/ blends, multisyllabic words, final consonants
Syntax	Past tense structure. Singular vs. plural	
Conjunctions	Compound sentences conjoined with "but/pero," "still/aún."	

Semantics	Days of the week, food vocabulary, descriptive terms (colors, number)
Sequencing	Caterpillar/butterfly life cycle, days of the week, counting
Wh- questions	What, who, where, when, why

Use songs with Familiar Sequence Stories

We like to use song and chants with familiar sequence stories. There are many songs that go along with most familiar sequences (e.g. days of the week, months of the year, counting, alphabet, etc). Songs are a great pre-reading activity to get children into the mindset of that specific sequence.

Keeping with the example, here are some songs we love that go great with *The Hungry Caterpillar* to teach the familiar sequences of the days of the week and numbers as well as telling the story:

Cinco patitos by Jose Luis Orozco	*Hungry Caterpillar* by The Learning Station
5 Little Ducks by The Learning Station	*Days of the Week/Dias de la semana* by Dr. Jean
Cinco elefantes by Stanley A. Lucero	*Today Is Sunday/Hoy es domingo* by Dr. Jean
Days of the Week by Twin Sisters	*Months of the Year/Meses del año* by Dr. Jean
Los dias de la semana by Jorge Anaya	*Five Little Monkeys/ Cinco monos pequeños* by Dr. Jean

Familiar Sequence Story Games

Familiar sequence stories are great for making predictions. The child can "guess" what is going to happen next because the story follows a structure that is familiar to them. This helps keep them excited and engaged because they have background knowledge that can help them to 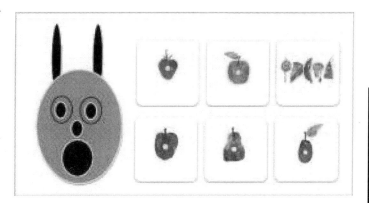 participate even more! The Hungry Caterpillar is the one book that people have developed a ton of games around. We created a following-directions activity where we build the caterpillar's head and then play a game to remember the sequence of the food that he eats. Students get to stuff the cards through the mouth to feed him the food.

Familiar Sequence Stories for Speech Therapy

	Title	Description of Story
	**Go Diego Go! To the Rescue! Al Rescate** **(Bilingual book)**	A bilingual (Spanish/English) board book with interactive, and voice output buttons. Why we like it: It's a great book for eliciting action words!
	**The Very Hungry Caterpillar** **La oruga muy hambrienta**	Plot: A colorful caterpillar moves his way through the life cycle, eating everything in his path. Why we like it: An Eric Carle classic and children's favorite, great book for teaching categories (food, colors), introducing the life cycle, comparing and contrasting and presenting days of the week and numbers.
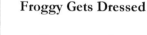 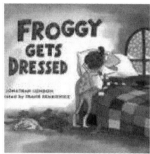	**Froggy Gets Dressed** **Froggy se viste**	Plot: A frog convinces his mom to let him go play in the snow, only to be reminded by her that he needs to put on more clothes each time he attempts to leave the house. Why we like it: Humorous story good for kids aged 3-5 targeting clothing, seasons, winter vocabulary and /r/.
 	**The Grouchy Ladybug** **La mariquita malhumorada**	Plot: The story of an ornery ladybug who gets involved in a series of tiffs with a succession of ever-larger animals. Why we like it: Beautiful illustrations and full of language targets: concepts of time, increasing sizes, cycle of day to night and great for teaching cooperation and expected/unexpected behavior.
	**Cookie's Week** **La semana de Cookie**	Plot: This story follows a mischievous kitten throughout each day of the week. Why we like it: Great book for preschoolers to teach the days of the week and also introduces fun topic of conversation of raising a pet which is a good language stimulation topic.

Ten Black Dots

Diez puntos negros

Plot: Simple illustrations with different configurations of dots that teaching counting.

Why we like it: An appealing book for toddlers that teaches counting skills in a fun and imaginative way; invites fun arts and crafts follow up activities to create different items/animals with black dots for language targets

Ten, Nine, Eight

Diez, Nueve, Ocho

Plot: A girl and her father count down to bedtime, teaching counting skills.

Why we like it: A Caldecott Honor book, this is a simple bedtime story that teaching counting and labeling skills in the context of the nursery; invites interactions and opportunities to make tangible connections

10 Little Rubber Ducks

10 patitos de goma

Plot: A story of 10 rubber ducks that are swept overboard off a cargo ship and travel to different parts of the world

Why we like it: Based on a true incident, this is another lovely book for teaching counting, colors, sequencing, and part-whole relationships

Today is Monday

Plot: Various animals march across each page, eating a different food/dish each day of the week.

Why we like it: Introduces animals, foods and days of the week for preschool aged children with a chant like verse that children could easily learn to sing along to. Great for targeting both language and phonology.

MAKING THERAPY GAMES

Pattern Stories

Pattern stories are the easiest to teach - best known - easiest to find books around. Scenes, characters, and phrases are repeated with minor variations such as in *Goldilocks and the Three Bears*.

Pattern stories are great for therapy because they:

- Can be easily used to teach and practice story retelling skills since they follow a predictable pattern and often include a predictable sequence.
- Include a pattern and new vocabulary words that often repeat, which can be helpful for targeting both semantic and phonological/articulation goals.
- Often make use of a familiar tone/inflection to which kids can chant along that can facilitate working on phonological and articulation skills – this is built-in repetition of target sounds and words – while still being fun!
- Are great books for using cloze procedures to further engage children in the story and teach new vocabulary, as the pattern repeats.
- Generally revolve around a theme or category that can be used to tie in with grade level curriculum and expand children's knowledge of basic concepts.

How to use Pattern Stories in Speech Therapy

As an example, here is one of our favorite pattern stories, and how we like to use it in therapy to target a variety of goals:

Froggy Gets Dressed/Froggy Se Viste

by Jonathan London

Goal:	English	Spanish
Articulation	/f, initial position, velar sounds /k/, /g/, /r/ blends	/r/ blends, /s/ blends, medial and final /s/, final /r/
Syntax	Present (play, sleep, wake, etc., and past tense sentence structures – regular and irregular (put, pulled, tugged, etc.)	Present tense structure and past tense structure (e.g. puso,)- Noun/verb agreement- singular vs. plural

Semantics	Clothing- socks, boots, hat, scarf, etc.; Weather terms – snow, cold, melt winter	Clothing- calcetines, botas, gorra, bufanda, etc.; Weather terms – nieve, frio, invierno, derritir
Strategies to learn new vocabulary	New terms- melt, tugged, etc.	New terms- derritir, calzar, atar, guantes, etc.
Wh- questions	What, who, where, when, why	Qué, quién, dónde, cuándo, por qué
Macrostructure- story elements, structure, organization of a narrative	Sequencing, story elements (characters, setting, problem, solution, initiating event, character intentions and desires, moral)	Sequencing, story elements (characters, setting, problem, solution, initiating event, character intentions and desires, moral)

Pattern Story Games

Pattern stories can be extremely helpful in reviewing familiar vocabulary and/or teaching new vocabulary. Like many predictable books, the same theme-based vocabulary will be repeated throughout the book. This gives children multiple opportunities to hear the words, repeat them and increase their understanding of new terms when used in different contexts within the book. This can be a great way to work on articulation and phonological targets and syntax and semantic goals as well.

To further cement their knowledge and use of desired vocabulary, using visuals from the books, we can create many of our own pre- and post-story activities to increase children's engagement with the material, and keep our lessons motivating and entertaining for little ones.

Below are a few ways we love to use a book to expand one lesson into many – and thus develop a mini-unit based around one story:

- Review and pre-teach new vocabulary using cards with visuals and/or including a surprise bag for smaller ones (have children guess what's inside the bag and then label and discuss items).
- Have children draw their own visuals for the story and label new vocabulary and practice target words – with *Froggy Gets Dressed* children can draw themselves and label what they are wearing that day.

- While presenting the story, we can use visuals from the book to enable kids to have a more active role in the story-telling process (i.e., puppets for characters, each one assigned to a child in group).

- Create a game board with story visuals to work on articulation target words or wh- questions as a post-story activity.

- Have students act out the story to work on their sequencing skills and use of temporal and sequential words.

Here is an example of an activity that we built in an manila folder for *Froggy Gets Dressed*. We get to practice naming body parts, name pieces of clothes, and most important to the children, laugh at his underwear.

Pattern Stories for Speech Therapy

Title	Description of Story

The Three Little Pigs

Los tres cerditos

Plot: The classic tale of three pigs who build their houses and encounter a troublesome wolf.

Why we like it: This bilingual version has both English and Spanish on each page and makes use of rhythm and rhyming. This story is great for working on sequencing and retelling, along with providing many articulation targets in both English and Spanish (/r/, /s/, /l/, /d/, /th/).

The Three Bears

Los tres osos

Plot: Classic story of Goldilocks misadventures exploring the three bears' home.

Why we like it: Using a story that many children are often familiar with can provide them with confidence in targeting retell skills. It also provides ample opportunities for language targets such as family members, size, object/function as well as expected behaviors.

The Three Billy Goats Gruff

Los tres chivitos

Plot: Three billy goats attempt to cross a bridge and outsmart a troublesome troll.

Why we like it: Another classic story that children may be familiar with provides opportunities for describing, comparing, contrasting and working on sequencing and story retelling skills.

The Carrot Seed

La semilla de zanahoria

Plot: A little boy plants a carrot seed and faithfully cares for it, waiting for it to grow, teaching patience to children.

Why we like it: Although this story is very simple, younger children can enjoy it for learning members of the family, steps to planting a seed, and labeling action words. This book can also serve as an introduction to teaching vegetables as well as targeting /r/ clusters in Spanish.

The Little Red Hen

La gallinita roja

Plot: The story of a hardworking hen who raises her wheat and bakes her bread while her neighbors idle by.

Why we like it: This is a nice version of the story with rhythm that children can chant to or fill in the blanks. Language targets include action words, labeling nouns, intro to planting/harvesting, and sequencing.

The Runaway Bunny

El conejito andarín

Plot: A bunny tells his mother he is going to run away and she lovingly describes how she will catch him.

Why we like it: From the same author and illustrator as Goodnight Moon, this story provides children with opportunities for labeling nouns (animals and places) and action words, describing, making predictions, and retelling a story with a structure and rhythm.

Seven Blind Mice

Siete ratones ciegos

Plot: A band of blind mice discover something near their pond and venture out to make guesses as to what it could be.

Why we like it: This story is wonderful for practice description of attributes, size, color, and shape, and guiding children in making predictions. They will be excited to find out what the creature is at the end of the story and whether their guesses matched up.

Goodnight Moon

Buenas noches luna

Plot: A classic bedtime story with goodnight wishes from a sleepy rabbit.

Why we like it: A soothing story for bedtime or a classroom routine (before naptime story), excellent for labeling, describing, increasing vocabulary and targeting 2- and 3-word phrases.

Question and Answer Stories

In "WH" question stories, the same or similar questions are repeated throughout the story such as in: *Brown Bear, Brown Bear, What Do You See?*

Question and answer stories are great for therapy because:

- The repetition of the same question, and often similar answers, helps increase students' participation with increased opportunities to practice a question or sentence structure.
- Question and answer stories provide great exposure to early developing question types.
- They provide an opportunity to learn conversational turn taking.
- For older students, non-fiction question and answer books provide an opportunity for students to do their own experiments and investigations, and write about them.
- You can easily include the scaffolding strategies of binary choice or picture reference, depending on the level of the child and the complexity of the book.

How to use Question and Answer Stories in Speech Therapy

Here is one of our favorite Question and Answer stories and examples of how we use it in therapy to target a variety of goals:

From Head to Toe/De la cabeza a los pies

by Eric Carle

Goal:	English	Spanish
Articulation	Velars /k/ and /g/, final consonants	Velars /k/ and /g/, multisyllabic words, /s/, clusters, final consonants

MAKING THERAPY GAMES

Syntax	First and second person (I and You), reflexive pronouns (Spanish), 3-5 word utterances
Semantics	Body parts, animals, action words
Wh- questions	What, who

Question and Answer Story Games

Question and answer stories are great because they overlap with all academic needs. Children need to be able to answer questions. Games give them the rare opportunity to be the person asking for a change. Here are some ideas for how to use Q&A books in your therapy and how to make your therapy extend outside of the therapy session. Then, an example for *From Head to Toe*.

- Short "plays" in a group setting, the children can take turns playing the different characters and taking turns asking each other the questions that were in the story.
- Create a "mini-book" for the child to take home and draw/write in their answers to questions pertinent to their life and their surroundings (example: Q: "Johnny, Johnny, what do you see?" A: "I see my doggy looking at me").
- Interview others in their environment using the question structures (example: "Mommy, I can turn my head. Can you do it?").
- Get outside the house or classroom! Go find all the things you can see, hear, body parts that can move, etc. and create a list to talk about.

From Head to Toe Competition

Making materials for Eric Carle's books is sometimes a waste of time because his pictures are so genuinely perfect. Remember when I said before that people who make books and games do not think like speech pathologists? He might be the one exception.

Take turns in your group or have a competition between who can remember and follow the directions from the pictures. Children can take turns "being the teacher" so that they can ask the questions too.

WH Question and Answer Stories for Speech Therapy

Title	Description of Story

How Big is a Pig?

Cerdota grandota

Plot: Visit the farm of opposites in this repetitive question and answer book to answer the mystery question: Just how big is a pig?

Why we like it: Simple repetitive story structure good for targeting opposites, describing, sizes, farm animals, and sounds (great for phonological awareness activities).

I Went Walking

Salí de paseo

Plot: A little boy goes for a walk and greets a series of animals on the way.

Why we like it: Great for practicing first person, past tense, animals, and simple sentence structure.

Brown Bear, Brown Bear, What Do You See?

Oso pardo, oso pardo, ¿qué ves ahí?

Plot: Successive animals 'pose' questions asking the reader to turn the page and see which animal is next.

Why we like it: Repetitive and rhythmic, this book for early readers is great for simple labeling, nouns, adjectives and colors, along with targeting 2-4 word combinations (I see...a horse/Yo veo...un caballo).

Are You My Mother?

¿Eres mi mamá?

Plot: A baby bird goes in search of his mother who has gone to look for something for him to eat.

Why we like it: With simple words and illustrations, this humorous book can be used to target vocabulary, interrogatives, and prediction making.

MAKING THERAPY GAMES

From Head to Toe

De la cabeza a los pies

Plot: Children imitate animals making different movements with body parts.

Why we like it: Good for targeting body parts, joint attention, following directions, and using first person.

Whose Mouse Are You?

¿De quién eres, ratoncito?

Plot: A mouse is looking for his family and receives a delightful surprise at the end of the story.

Why we like it: Lots of rhyming makes it great for targeting articulation and phonological skills for young children.

Panda Bear, Panda Bear, What Do You See?

Oso panda, oso panda, ¿qué ves allí?

Also, Polar Bear, Polar Bear, What Do You Hear?

Plot: Various animals are featured in this follow up to Brown Bear, as a tribute to endangered species.

Why we like it: A another beginner book for labeling nouns, attributes, action words and practicing 2-3 word phrases.

The Very Busy Spider

La araña muy ocupada

Plot: Various farm animals try to distract a spider that is busy spinning her web but the spider continues her work.

Why we like it: Introducing animals, places, and actions. Great for working on sounds: English (/s/ clusters, medial /s/) Spanish: /r/, /ene/, medial /d/).

The Bus For Us

Nuestro autobus

Plot: A little's girl's first day at school and first ride on the school bus.

Why we like it: Introduces transportation; good for working on categories, school vocabulary; first day of school book. Good opportunities for the /s/.

Repetition of Phrase Stories

In a repetition of phrase story the word order of a phrase or sentence often has a cadence that slows downs, speeds up, or even rhymes. A good example is *Goodnight Moon/Buenas noches luna.*

Repetition of phrase stories are great for therapy because:

- The repetition of wording from the story allows young readers to participate and/or chant along with the story, further engaging them in the chain of events.
- Are especially conducive to teaching inferencing and prediction-making skills for children before they can read on their own.
- Children can anticipate what's coming next, which develops increased confidence in establishing basic reading skills.
- The repetition built into the story can easily provide numerous opportunities for exposing children to new syntactical rules.
- The repeated phrases can be very helpful in practicing a targeted speech sound or phonological process.
- Familiarity and predictability guide children to develop increased understanding and comprehension of material, which is why children will often beg us to re-read a book or continue with a familiar series – great for building vocabulary and helps us support academic skills at the same time!

How to use Repetition of Phrase Stories in Speech Therapy

Here is one of our favorite repetition of phrase stories and examples of how we use it in therapy to target a variety of goals:

Bear on a Bike/Oso en bicicleta:

by Stella Blackstone

Goal:	English	Spanish
Articulation	Bilabials /b/ and /p/, velars /k/ and /g/, final /r/, /ng/ in present progressive action words (i.e., 'swimming', 'riding')	Medial and final /s/, consonant clusters with /r/ and /l/, medial /d/ in present progressive forms (i.e., 'nadando', 'montando')
Syntax	Present progressive forms, future tense,3-5 word utterances	
Semantics	Transportation vocabulary (car, boat, plane, etc.), categories (fruit, animals, places), action words	
Wh- questions	What, who, where, when questions	

Repetition of Phrase Story Games

Bear on a Bike/Oso en bicicleta, is actually one book from a series of beautifully illustrated and written books that revolve around a bear's journeys around and outside of his town. This particular book fits neatly into the repetition of phrase category, and also is wonderful for targeting many basic concepts and vocabulary. *Bear on a Bike* contrasts travel by land, water, and air, which lends itself to creating a set of activities that help children compare and categorize means of transportation.

Transportation Bingo

We used the transportation vocabulary from the book to create sets of individualized Bingo cards. Bingo cards can be used in two ways:

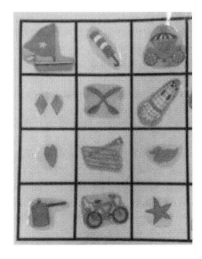

1) Play bingo normally having the children call out the vocabulary or produce phrases in order to get a chip to cover it up: "I have a bike."
2) Give children the cards while the story is being read to make them pay attention very well. They cover up the item as they appear in the story.

For vocabulary-themed stories, you can produce and play the game as part of the pre-reading activities to give the children a rich understanding of the new words before the story even begins.

Repetition of Phrase Stories for Speech Therapy

Title	Description of Story

Do You Want to Be My Friend?

Plot: A little mouse meets many animals while bravely looking for a friend.

Why we like it: A simple story with not much text, this is a nice book for teaching retell and predicting skills.

Is Your Mama a Llama?

¿Tu mamá es una llama?

Plot: Six baby animals help a baby llama find his mother.

Why we like it: Repetitive, Q&A, rhyming, this short story is good for presenting second person, working on sounds and phonological skills and developing prediction skills.

Polar Bear, Polar Bear, What Do You Hear?

Oso polar, oso polar, ¿qué es ese ruido?

Also, Brown Bear, Brown Bear, What Do You See?

Plot: Another story in a similar format to Brown Bear, each animal introduces the consecutive animal and sound it makes.

Why we like it: Similar to its predecessor, it is helpful for working on expanding vocabulary, action words and first person utterances.

Bear On a Bike

Oso en bicicleta

Plot: A bear, a boy and a dog travel many lands, looking for adventure.

Why we like it: A wonderful book for Pre-k and Kindergarten-aged kids to introduce categories (transportation, places, foods), sequence and time concepts, and plenty of articulation targets (/r/ clusters, /s/ in all positions).

MAKING THERAPY GAMES

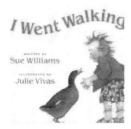

I Went Walking

Salí de paseo

Plot: A little boy goes for a walk and greets a series of animals on the way.

Why we like it: Great for first person, past tense, animals, simple sentence structure.

Jump, Frog, Jump!

Salta ranita, salta!

Plot: A traveling frog evades his prey hopping from page to page.

Why we like it: Repetitive, cumulative story to use for articulation and phonological processes (English: /r/ clusters, Spanish initial /rr/ and /s/.

Mortimer

Mortimer - Español

Plot: A little boy won't go to sleep at night and keeps his family up.

Why we like it: A repetitive format that kindergarten aged students will enjoy - great book to get children chanting and singing, could be used for a student with fluency and/or phonological impairments.

No, Titus, No!

No, Tito, no!

Plot: A fox and other animals help a dog understand his role on the farm.

Why we like it: Helpful for teaching young children their role at home, great for working on labeling, describing actions, and teaching pragmatics skills.

The Three Billy Goats Gruff

Los tres chivitos

Plot: A lovely version of the classic tale of the three billy goats who have to evade a troll to cross a bridge.

Why we like it: Easily adapted to almost any goal and easy comparison to other stories.

Rhyme Stories

Using a story that rhymes is like driving your car on cruise control. The rhyme takes over the cadence, intonation, and length so we can focus on the content. Communication requires expectation. Someone says something, and we respond. Someone asks a question that we then answer. The rhyme naturally delivers this expectation through the rhymed syllable sound or word.

Rhyme stories can be as short and simple as *Humpty Dumpty* or as advanced as a full storybook poem like *Room on a Broom.*

Rhyme Stories are great for therapy because:

- You can find simple to complex rhymes to easily match even the most profound communication deficits.
- Many students have familiarity with rhymes.
- Rhymes are present in all cultures.
- Rhymes easily enable the production of longer utterances by employing meter and relying on repetitious phrasing.
- There are many opportunities to use past, present, future, and even conditional tense.
- Rhythms present in the rhymes create natural opportunities for whole body and kinesthetic movements.
- Phonological syllable-building is aided by clapping or tapping the beat.
- Many rhymes have moral or ethical themes embedded in their message.

How to use Rhyme Stories in Speech Therapy

The Gruffalo is a great example of the power of rhyme. It is a full text story including location, characters, problems, and solutions. A mouse invents a monster to scare off other animals who want to eat him but winds up meeting an actual Gruffalo in the end. Let's use it as an example for what we can accomplish in speech therapy.

The Gruffalo / El Gruffalo

by Julia Donaldson

Goal:	English	Spanish
Articulation	/r/, /s/high use of fricatives	/r/, /r/ blends, /s/
Syntax	Possessive pronouns, conditional tense. Descriptions of body parts and inferencing on the part of the animals as to what would happen to them if they met the Gruffalo.	Past tense structure, especially irregular verbs (e.g. tiene, fue, vió, era)
Semantics	Body parts- eyes, teeth, claws and other invented body parts. Multiple animals, forest words.	Body parts- ojos, dientes, garras, etc.
Wh- questions	"Where" use every other page.	"Qué" use every other page.
Macrostructure- story elements, structure, organization of a narrative	Sequencing, story elements (characters, setting, problem, solution, initiating event, character intentions and desires, moral)	

Rhyme Story Games and Activities.

Rhymes = action and most rhymes have been around for a long time. Do an internet image search for YOUR BOOK + ACTIVITY and you will find a treasure trove of masks, games, songs, catapults, to adapt for therapy. The sky is truly the limit. For *The Gruffalo*, you can even go to www.Gruffalo.com! Some of our favorites for the Gruffalo include:

- Anatomy charts for the Gruffalo's amazing body parts.
- Lunch bag puppets to eat the animals with
- Animal story-sequencing activities
- Pantomime hand movements for each repeated rhyme:
    o terrible tusks
    o terrible claws
    o terrible teeth
    o in his terrible jaws.

Rhyme Books for Speech Therapy

	Title	Description of Story

Green Eggs and Ham

Huevos verdes con jamon

Plot: Sam-I-am persistently asks: "Do you like green eggs and ham?" through a traveling, rhyming story.

Why we like it: This book as memorable and unmistakable characters and signature rhymes. Also helpful with reading goals.

Chicka Chicka Boom Boom

Plot: 26 characters of the alphabet make their way to the top of a coconut tree before the tree bends from the weight.

Why we like it: The book adds familiar order using the alphabet to the rhyme which makes it easy to follow and memorize. The children can relate to everyone wanted to join in on the fun but there being too many!

Sheep in a Jeep

Plot: A flock of hapless sheep drive through the country in this rhyming picture book.

Why we like it: Lots of action words and onomatopoeia. High use of fricative sounds and kids love watching what all goes wrong when the sheep try to drive.

I Ain't Gonna Paint No More!

Plot: A child paints the walls, then the ceiling, then himself before his mother comes in.

Why we like it. This book rhymes to the tune of "It Ain't Gonna Rain No More." It is a nice change of pace grammatically. Lots of opportunities to describe colors, do painting projects, and discuss behavior.

Tanka Tanka Skunk!

Plot: This a rhyming book about rhyming. Skunk and Tanka use inventive words to create a beat on drums.

Why we like it: This book is really fun and uses made up words. It helps for utterance expansion and kids love to tap the beat out on the table top so it helps with producing more syllables.

MAKING THERAPY GAMES

Llama Llama Red Pajama

La llama llama rojo pijama

Plot: Baby Llama turns bedtime into an all-out llama drama when he wants his mama.

Why we like it: Good way to express wants and needs, deal with fears, and make requests. Good use of plural words and initial /r/ words.

Giraffes Can't Dance

Las jirafas no pueden bailar

Plot: Gerald the giraffe's legs are too skinny and his neck is too long to be able to dance but then he gets up the courage.

Why we like it: It teaches acceptance of yourself and others and also teaches discovering unknown abilities. Great book for description, body parts, animal vocabulary, and self-esteem.

Frog on a Log

Plot: Cats sit on mats, hares sit on chairs, mules sit on stools, and frogs sit on logs. Each animal's designated seat rhymes with that animal's name. The cat explains: "It's about doing the right thing." The frog does not want to!

Why we like it: Power to the little people for standing up for what they want! Great rhyming, sequencing, and categorization.

The Gruffalo

El Gruffalo

Plot: Mouse goes for a walk in a dangerous forest. To scare off his enemies he invents tales of a fantastical creature called the Gruffalo which turns out to be real.

Why we like it: Great repetitive rhyme. Filled with almost all target sounds. Amazing description, forest and animal vocabulary.

The Lorax

El Lorax

Plot: The Lorax protects the planet from mindless progress. A timely message and a bonus that most kids know the plot from the movie.

Why we like it: Full of /r/, /l/, /s/ sounds and clusters. Lots of questions and answers and opportunities to make prediction based on behavior.

Song Stories

A song story is a story that contains rhyming words, refrains, or patterns that are used throughout the story. Song stories can be a wonderful addition to our therapy as they are an extremely motivating tool and provide greater opportunity for engagement for little ones. Such as *Wheels on the Bus.*

Song stories are great for therapy because:

- They make therapy so much fun and will make children even more excited and engaged about participating in therapy.
- They are conducive to teaching speech paired with gestures which can be incredibly helpful for children who are working on gaining basic vocabulary.
- They can easily be used to target early developing sounds and provide younger children with more repetition.
- They can be a great way to introduce a new theme or topic and provide them with exposure to new vocabulary.
- Children with whom songs and song stories are used frequently will begin to anticipate the inclusion of a song and can be motivated by choosing one of their favorites.
- Making use of melody and rhythm within speech and language therapy has been shown to be a successful strategy with students who have fluency impairments to boost confidence, apraxia to increase length of utterance, and autism to increase joint attention and engage the student.

How to use Song Stories in Speech Therapy

As an example, here is one of our favorite song stories, and how we like to use it in therapy to target a variety of goals:

Five Little Monkeys Jumping on the Bed/Cinco monitos brincando en la cama

by Eileen Christelow

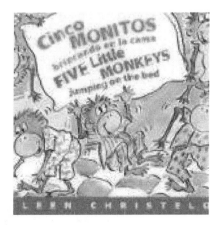

185

Goal:	English	Spanish
Articulation	/f/, /j/, final /s/ (monkeys)	/k/, /m/, /s/, /r/ clusters (brincaron)
Syntax	Prepositions (English – on, off; Spanish – en, de)	
	Negatives	
	Simple past tense (ex. English: jumped, bumped; Spanish- cayó, pegó, llamó)	
	Irregular past tense (ex. English: said, fell; Spanish – pusieron, dijeron	
	Present progressive (English – jumping), compound sentences	
Semantics	Bedtime vocabulary/routines	
	Quantitative concepts – numbers/counting 1-5; (all, some, none)	
	Feelings (happy, sad, worried, mad)	
Pragmatics	Expected behaviors	
	Consequences of actions/Cause and effect	
Wh- questions	What, who, where, when, why	

Song Story Games and Activities

Using song books is all about singing, acting, making noises, and including as many different sensory activities as possible. The song and singing obviously creates auditory stimuli. Song books become powerful when we add in tactile, visual, and kinesthetic feedback. For many of our song stories we create puppets or faces so that the children can act out the story or have the characters sing with them. As an example, here is a folder activity made out of clothespins so that the monkeys can fall off the bed. This is also a paper plate monkey face that can be used to sing the songs.

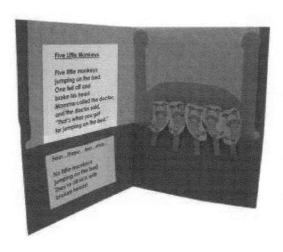 

Great during- and post-reading activities to go along with *Five Little Monkeys Jumping on the Bed:*

- Provide each child with a picture or token manipulative monkey to use while the song and story are being presented along with a bed so that children can join in while the story is being told.

- Give children opportunities to learn the story and chant or sing along by presenting the story over a number of days – re-reading/reviewing stories so that children become familiar with them is a wonderful way to target articulation and new vocabulary. Use purposeful pauses in the story to allow children to 'fill in the blank.'

- Have children create a monkey face crafted from paper plates to work on following instructions and requesting necessary items. The monkey face could be converted into a mask with a popsicle stick and children could act out the story after reading to practice a simple story retell.

- Using the story as a starting point, collaborate and create a bedtime social story for younger children to take home and use with parents or create a chart including expected and unexpected bedtime routine behaviors.

- Use a rhyming activity to work on phonological and speech sound goals with students using words from the story – have children clap along and practice rhyming words or come up with words on their own.

Song Books for Speech Therapy

Title	Description of Story
 **Old MacDonald Had a Farm** **La granja del viejo Juan**	Plot: This classic children's song book version with illustrations and opportunities for interaction. Why We Like It: Great for early childhood aged children, both versions of this book have built in opportunities for the children to interact with the book, name and describe animals and practice /l/, /f/ and bilabials in English and /l/, /r/ clusters and bilabials in Spanish.
 **Lizard's Song** **La canción del lagarto**	Plot: A simple songbook about a lizard willing to share and finding out why it's important to be yourself. Why we like it: A light-hearted story with a valuable lesson, this rhyming songbook is appropriate for children aged 3-5 to teach describing and phonological skills.
 **Cada Niño/Every Child: A Bilingual Songbook for Kids**	Plot: This book includes 11 traditional and original songs in both English and Spanish celebrating Hispanic culture. Why we like it: Includes many familiar and new songs for children aged 3-6, with predictable rhyming songs for working on phonemic awareness skills, identifying categories (family, food, animals), and many sounds in both languages.
 **The Wheels on the Bus** **Las ruedas del autobus**	Plot: The school bus travels through town in this storybook version of the classic song. Why we like it: This book provides wonderful opportunities for following directions and working on many sounds, including bilabials and velars, in both languages.

Five Little Monkeys Jumping on the Bed

Cinco monitos brincando en la cama

Plot: Kids will love this silly tale of monkeys jumping on the bed, and each one's successive consequences.

Why we like it: A rhyming and counting book to sing along to, this story can be used to teach /f/, /l/, and bilabials in English and /s/, /r/ clusters and bilabials in Spanish.

The Bilingual Book of Rhymes, Songs, Stories and Fingerplays: Over 450 Spanish/English Selections

Plot: This extensive collection of rhymes, songs and stories combined, includes mostly traditional English nursery rhymes and stories translated to Spanish.

Why we like it: Great tool for building vocabulary and sounds for speech development.

Diez Deditos and Other Play Rhymes and Action Songs from Latin America

Bilingual Book

Plot: A bilingual collection of finger rhymes and action songs put together by wonderful children's musician, Jose Luis Orozco. Children will enjoy singing and moving with the songs and rhymes.

Why we like it: Songs with actions paired with words give children another input to learn sounds and syllables.

The Frog Was Singing

Cantaba la rana

Bilingual Book

Plot: Another beautiful collection of traditional Spanish folksongs from Latin America in both English and Spanish, also includes music for piano.

Why We Like It: Rhyming, poetic verses provide an introduction for children to songs in Spanish and English; could be used to work on /r/, /s/, /k/, /g/ in Spanish, and /s/, /k/, /g/ and /r/ clusters in English.

A la rueda rueda - Traditional Latin American Folk Songs for Children

Bilingual Book

Plot: A collection of 34 songs for early childhood through elementary school aged children with an accompanying CD.

Why we like It: This songbook includes beautiful illustrations with reproducible pages and games for children with English translations and a pronunciation guide. Helpful for supporting development of articulation skills.

For more great song books visit our **Best Books for Speech Therapy** *page: https://bilinguistics.com/books-for-speech-therapy/*

MAKING THERAPY GAMES

Great Resources for Predictable Books

I don't know about you, but knowing about predictable books helped me understand WHY and HOW to choose books for speech therapy. If you search for "Predictable Books" on the internet you will find a ton of resources. Of course, all the book lists are in English. If you search "Predictable Books Spanish" do you know what you'll find? Crickets. Many of the books listed do have Spanish counterparts though.

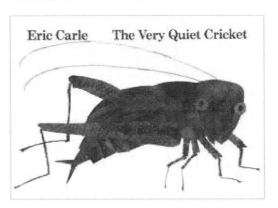

Searching for Predictable Books

Here are some awesome website resources on predictable books with English suggestions that you can use with your English-speaking kiddos.

Good Reads

Pros

Provides a list of predictable books.

Cons

English only. Does not provide information on the type of book, theme, or genre.

Educational Resource Center

Pros

Provides definition of predictable books- provides a list of books by author, including the type of predictable book.

Cons

English only-Difficult to navigate unless you know the exact author you are searching for.

Charlotte Mason Approach

Pros

Provides a list of predictable books.

Cons

English only. Does not provide information on the type of book, theme or genre. Includes some links to purchase books through Amazon.

Scholastic

Pros

This is a site focused on Predictable books. Search for books by reading level, DRA, grade level equivalent, or Guided Reading level (A-Z- Includes type of predictable books, tells genre of books, has book summaries, has short clips of text from books, identifies the themes/subjects in the book (cooking, seasons), and has free teaching resources to go along with the books.

Cons

English only. Scholastic has a great bilingual book list but without all the information as the English books. There is also no definition of types of predictable books

Kaplan Early Learning

Pros

Provides a list of bilingual books, provides the guided reading level

Cons

Only 9 books are listed, does not provide information on the type of book, theme or genre

Nellie Edge

Pros

Provides a list of popular predictable books in English

Cons

Does not provide information on the type of book, theme or genre

University of Wisconsin Polk Library

Pros

Provides a list of books by author, including the type of predictable book. You can get a Google "preview" of the inside of the book. After clicking through a few links, you can eventually get to a place to purchase a copy

Cons

English only, does not include reading level, concepts to target, books link to the university library only; no option to purchase

Great Books for Literacy-Based Intervention

What Makes a Book Great for Speech Therapy?

Many SLPs love books and we tend to gravitate to our same favorite books year after year. If it is not obvious by this point, we love children's books.

But why do we choose the books we choose? Why some but not all?

As it turns out, as SLPs we look at books very differently (and are often much more picky) than educators, authors, librarians, and parents. Working with bilingual children, the ante is upped even more because the resources are limited. This got us all thinking about what makes a book seem "good" to our SLP brains.

Key criteria that are important in selecting successful books for speech therapy.

- Ample opportunities for the child to participate
- The ability to work on specific goals in the context of the book
- A structure that enables easier story-telling
- Opportunities for practice of specific sounds
- Obvious sequencing
- Good Illustrations
- Intrigue that allows us to ask "what if…" and inferencing questions.

We divided the books in this section by common goals and age/grade. You could make an argument that some books go into different (or many) categories. However, these are how we search for these books most often. When applicable, we included the Spanish title.

Appendix I: Books by Age and Grade

Best Books for Young Children

Black and White by Tana Hoban

Blue Hat, Green Hat by Sandra Boynton

Brown Bear, Brown Bear by Bill Martin, Jr.

The Going to Bed Book by Sandra Boynton

Goodnight Moon by Margaret Wise Brown and Clement Hurd

Good Night, Gorilla by Peggy Rathman

Guess How Much I Love You by Sam McBratney

Love You Forever by Robert Munsch

More, More, More Said the Baby by Vera B. Williams

Whistle for Willie by Ezra Jack Keats

Yum Yum Dim Sum by Amy Wilson Sanger

Books for Speech Therapy – Elementary Level

Title	Age Range	Description
The Snowy Day	Age Range: 2+	Follow Peter as he finds the wonderful things a snowy day has to offer.
Heckedy Peg	Age Range: 4-7	Seven children are transformed into food by a witch when they did not listen to their mother.
Tuesday	Age Range: 4-7	This wordless picture book depicts what can happen when frogs begin to take flight one Tuesday morning.

Title	Age Range	Description
Where the Wild Things Are	Age Range: 4-8	An iconic book about a little boy who goes on an adventure and encounters beasts and creatures created by a child's awesome imagination.
Henry's Freedom Box	Age Range: 4-8	Henry Brown is a slave, and the outcomes of his life are a direct outcome of this fact. He finds freedom when he mails himself in a box to the North.
A Chair for My Mother	Age Range: 4-10	Rosa, her mother, and grandmother, with the support of their community, save their coins to buy a chair following a fire that destroyed their home.
Alexander and the Terrible, Horrible, No Good, Very Bad Day	Age Range: 6-9	Waking up with gum in his hair, Alexander knew it was going to be a bad day. Follow him as he encounters mishaps throughout his day.
Martin's Big Words	Age Range: 5-8	Follow a young Martin as he learns about the importance of words, civil rights and helping people . Readers will learn about the life events that contributed to Dr. Martin Luther King's life and death.
Those Shoes	Age Range: 5-8	Jeremy wants a pair of shoes that his Grandma cannot afford. After a serendipitous find at a thrift store, Jeremy buys a too-small pair of *those shoes*. The events that follow teach the reader about the important things in life—warmth, family and compassion.
King Bidgood's in the Bathtub	Age Range: 4-7	Various creative people of the king's court try to get him to leave his bathtub.

Books for Speech Therapy – Secondary Level

Title	Age Range	Description
Danny Dragonbreath	Age Range: 7-12	(Graphic Novel) This book series is about Danny Dragon and his friends as they partake in adventures.
Sir Cumference	Age Range : 8-12	The neighboring kingdom is threatening war, and King Arthur, with the help of geometry and witty characters (e.g,. Sir Cumference, Lady Di of Ameter), finds a way to peace. This book series uses humor and math-based vocabulary and concepts tell a fun and humorous story.
The Arrival by Shaun Tan	Age Range: 9+	(Wordless Graphic Novel) Through beautiful drawings, the reader follows the tale of a man who leaves his family to find a better home and life. Strange and unexpected adventures ensue in the new land as he learns about the compassion of strangers.
Tales of the Fourth Grade Nothing	Age Range: 8-12	Peter must constantly deal with his little brother Fudge. Thankfully, his turtle Dribble understands Peter's woes until an expected event changes everything.
The Phantom Tollbooth	Age Range: 8-12	Upon entry into a tollbooth that appears in his room, Milo discovers that life is, in actuality, not dull.
A Wrinkle in Time	Age Range: 10-14	Meg Murry and her brother Charles Wallace have not seen their father, a scientist for the government. With the help of some unique characters, they go on an adventure to find their father by traveling through a tesseract, a wrinkle in time.

Appendix II: Books by Therapy Goals

Goal: Describing

English Title	Spanish Title	Description
Why Mosquitos Buzz in People's Ears	*Por qué zumban los mosquitos en los oídos de la gente*	A mosquito tells a lie to an iguana and sets off a series of events. It is a 'fable-like' story.
The Snowy Day	*Un día de nieve*	This is a young boy's experience on a snowy day. Peter explores and enjoys the snow in many ways.
The Mixed-Up Chameleon	*El camaleon camaleonico*	When a chameleon realizes it can change, it adds body parts and colors from many animals at once.
The Little Old Lady Who Wasn't Afraid of Anything	*La viejecita que no le tenía miedo a nada*	The story of a lady who never gets scared, until one night she is followed by haunted clothes that form a scarecrow.
Go Away, Big Green Monster!	*¡Fuera de aquí, horrible monstruo verde!*	While turning the pages of this die-cut book, a big green monster grows then disappears.
The Gigantic Turnip	*El nabo gigante*	A farmer and his wife find a giant turnip in their garden that requires cooperation from all the animals on the farm.
The Gingerbread Man	*El hombre de pan de jengibre*	A couple makes a child out of gingerbread. He comes to life and escapes them.
Where the Wild Things Are	*Donde viven los monstrous*	A boy imagines himself traveling to a far away place, makes unlikely friends and learns to appreciate what he has.
A Chair for My Mother	*Un sillón para mi mamá*	A family must work together with their community to rebuild their home after a fire.

Goal: Action Verbs

English Title	Spanish Title	Description
Cookie's Week	*La semana de cookie*	This story follows a mischievous kitten throughout each day of the week.
Go Diego Go! To the Rescue!/ ¡Al rescate!		A bilingual (Spanish/English) board book with interactive, and voice output buttons.
If You Give a Pig a Pancake	*Si le das un panqueque a una cerdita*	A pig is given a pancake leading to a chain of comical consequences.
If You Give a Moose a Muffin	*Si le das un panecillo a un alce*	A surprise guest invites himself in and takes advantage of a boy's hospitality in an entertaining way.
If You Give a Mouse a Cookie	*Si le das una galletita a un ratón*	When a mouse invites himself into the house and is given a cookie, a number of entertaining consequences ensue.
Knuffle Bunny	*El conejito Knuffle*	On an errand to the laundromat, Trixie loses her beloved stuffed bunny, and he gets into mischief left alone.
Froggy Gets Dressed	*Froggy se viste*	A frog goes to play in the snow, only to be reminded by his mother that he needs to put on more clothes each time.
The Little Old Lady Who Wasn't Afraid of Anything	*La viejecita que no le tenía miedo a nada*	The story of a lady who never gets scared, until one night she is followed by haunted clothes that form a scarecrow.
The Gingerbread Man	*El hombre de pan de jengibre*	A couple makes a child out of gingerbread. He comes to life and escapes them.

GREAT STORYBOOKS

Goal: Naming

English Title	Spanish Title	Description
Today Is Monday	*Hoy es lunes*	Animals march across each page, eating a different food each day of the week.
Ten Little Rubber Ducks	*Diez patitos amarillos*	10 rubber ducks are swept overboard off a cargo ship and travel to different parts of the world.
Ten, Nine, Eight	*Diez, Nueve, Ocho*	A girl and her father count down to bedtime, teaching counting skills.
The Grouchy Ladybug	*La mariquita malhumorada*	The story of a ladybug who picks fights with animals much larger than herself.
The Very Hungry Caterpillar	*La oruga muy hambrienta*	A caterpillar moves his way through the life cycle, eating everything in his path.
The Mitten	*El mitón*	A boy's grandmother makes him mittens. He goes for a walk and loses one in the snow.
There Was an Old Lady Who Swallowed a Fly		An old lady swallows one animal after another to catch the preceding one.
Bear about Town	*Oso en la ciudad*	Every day, Bear strolls through his town to do something special.
Bear on a Bike	*Oso en bicicleta*	Bear on a Bike travels around the world by bike, train, raft, boat and even hot-air balloon, and a special night-time journey.
Bear in Sunshine	*Oso bajo el sol*	Whether it's raining, sunny, hot or cold, Bear always knows how to have fun.
Brown Bear, Brown Bear, What Do You See?	*Oso pardo, oso pardo, ¿qué ves ahí?*	A big happy frog, a plump purple cat, a handsome blue horse, and a soft yellow duck-- all parade across the pages of this delightful book.

Goal: Following Directions

English Title	Spanish Title	Description
Ten Black Dots	*Diez puntos negros*	Simple illustrations with different configurations of dots that teaching counting.
Lilly's Purple Plastic Purse	*Lily y su bolso de plastico morado*	Lilly brings her purple plastic purse and its treasures to school and can't wait until sharing time, Mr. Slinger confiscates her prized possessions.
Howard B. Wigglebottom Learns to Listen		Howard B. Wigglebottom is a curious rabbit who just doesn't listen!
Strega Nona	*Strega Nona*	When Strega Nona leaves him alone with her magic pasta pot, Big Anthony is determined to show the townspeople how it works.
Don't Let the Pigeon Drive the Bus!	*¡No dejes que la paloma conduzca el autobus!*	When a bus driver takes a break from his route, a very unlikely volunteer springs up to take his place-a pigeon!
Olivia the Spy		Everyone's favorite pig is about to have a birthday…but will her penchant for eavesdropping lead to more than presents?
From Head to Toe	*De la cabeza a los pies*	This book invites kids to imitate animal movements. Watching giraffes bend their necks or monkeys wave their arms is fun, but nothing could be better than joining in.
Oink, Oink Benny		Benny, an incorrigible little pig, falls into a mud hole after disregarding his mother's instructions. This story, told with spare text and expressive pictures, will have your kids giggling while it teaches them the consequences of not listening.

GREAT STORYBOOKS

Goal: Sequencing

English Title	Spanish Title	Description
The Three Little Pigs	*Los tres cerditos*	The three pigs find out whose house really is the strongest when they each stand up to the big, bad wolf.
The Three Billy Goats Gruff	*Los tres chivitos*	The Three Billy Goats Gruff live on a hillside and they have to cross an old bridge guarded by a terrible troll.
Goldilocks and the Three Bears	*Ricitos de oro y los tres osos*	The three bears return home and realize that a curious girl has made herself at home in their cottage.
Five Little Monkeys Jumping on the Bed	*Cinco monitos brincando en la cama*	Five Little Monkeys Jumping on the Bed. Title kind of says it all.
The Very Hungry Caterpillar	*La oruga muy hambrienta*	The very hungry caterpillar literally eats his way through the pages of the book and through a whole series of food.
Are You My Mother?	*¿Eres tú mi mamá?*	A baby bird goes in search of his mother and meets all sorts of animals along the way.
There's a Wocket in My Pocket!	*Hay un molillo en mi bolsillo!*	*There's a Wocket in My Pocket* is filled with bizarre creatures and rhymes: the nupboard in the cupboard, ghairs beneath the stairs, and the bofa on the sofa!
Brown Bear, Brown Bear, What Do You See?	*Oso pardo, oso pardo, ¿qué ves ahí?*	A big happy frog, a plump purple cat, a handsome blue horse, and a soft yellow duck-- all parade across the pages of this delightful book.
Froggy Gets Dressed	*Froggie se viste*	Rambunctious Froggy hops out into the snow for a winter frolic but is called back by his mother to put on some necessary articles of clothing.

Goal: Asking and Answering Questions

English Title	Spanish Title	Description
Snowmen at Night		Have you ever built a snowman and discovered the next day that his grin has gotten a little crooked, or his tree-branch arms have moved? And you've wondered . . . what do snowmen do at night? This delightful wintertime tale reveals all!
Mr. Brown Can Moo, Can You?		Mr. Brown is a sound-making wonder! He can *hoo hoo* like an owl and *buzz buzz* like a bee.
Brown Bear, Brown Bear, What Do You See?	*Oso pardo, oso pardo, ¿qué ves ahí?*	A big happy frog, a plump purple cat, a handsome blue horse, and a soft yellow duck-- all parade across the pages of this delightful book.
Polar Bear, Polar Bear, What Do You Hear?	*Oso polar, oso polar, ¿qué es ese ruido?*	This book uses movement and animal conservation through rhythmic text and vibrant images,
Are You My Mother?	*¿Eres tú mi mamá?*	A baby bird goes in search of his mother asking questions of other animals.
How Big Is a Pig?	*Cerdota grandota*	With a clever, repetitive text, How Big Is a Pig? follows in the footsteps of a cheerful piglet as he takes you on a trail around the farmyard.
Peek-A Who?		Colorful pictures and simple rhyming texts help children guess what's peeking through the die-cut windows in these two fun board books.
There Was an Old Lady Who Swallowed a Fly!	*Un dia una señora se tragó una mosca*	With rhyming text and great illustrations, this old familiar song makes us continually ask: "Why?"

GREAT STORYBOOKS

Appendix III: Books by Popular Curriculum Topics

Topic	English Title	Spanish Title
All About Me / Todo acerca de mi	*Froggy Gets Dressed* *From Head to Toe* *Go Away, Big Green Monster!* *My Five Senses*	*Froggy se viste* *De la cabeza a los pies* *Fuera de aquí, horrible monstruo verde!* *Mis cinco sentidos* *Yo soy especial*
School / La escuela	*Emily Elizabeth Goes to School* *Franklin Goes to School* *Froggie Goes to School* *David Goes to School* *If You Take a Mouse to School*	*Emily Elizabeth va a la escuela* *Franklin va a la escuela* *El primer día de la escuela* *Froggie va a la escuela* *David va al colegio* *Si llevas un ratón a la escuela*
Animals / Los animals	*Brown Bear, Brown Bear, What Do You See?* *From Head to Toe* *I Went Walking* *Animals* *Let's Go to the Farm*	*¿Oso pardo, oso pardo, qué ves allí?* *De la cabeza a los pies* *Salí de paseo* *Animales* *Vamos a la granja*
Family / La familia	*We're Going on a Bear Hunt* *Does a Kangaroo Have a Mother Too?* *Froggy Bakes a Cake* *My family and I* *Bear's Busy Family*	*Vamos a casar un oso* *¿El canguro tiene mamá?* *Mi familia y yo* *La familia ocupada de Oso*
Fall / El otoño	*We're Going on a Leaf Hunt* *Leaf Man* *I See Fall* *Leaves in Fall* *The Little Old Lady Who Was Not Afraid of Anything*	 *Veo el otoño* *Las hojas en otoño* *El circulo de las calabazas* *La viejecita que no le tenía miedo de nada*
Growing things/Cosas que crecen	*The Carrot Seed* *Growing Vegetable Soup* *The Gigantic Turnip* *Jack and the Beanstalk* *I'm a Seed*	*La semilla de zanahoria* *A sembrar sopa de verduras* *El nabo gigante* *Juan y los frijoles mágicos* *Soy una semilla*

Food/Comida	*Stone Soup*	*Sopa de piedras*
	The Gigantic Turnip	*El nabo gigante*
	The Very Hungry Caterpillar	*La oruga muy hambrienta*
	The Gingerbread Man	*El hombre de pan de jengibre*
Weather / El clima	*The Weather*	*El tiempo*
	What Should I Wear Today?	*¿Qué ropa me pongo hoy?*
	Bear in Sunshine	*Oso bajo sol*
	Elmer's Weather	*Elmer y el tiempo*
	Iguanas in the Snow	*Iguanas en la nieve*
	The Lizard and the Sun	*La lagartija y el sol*
Places We Go / Lugares donde vamos	*Bear About Town*	*Oso en la ciudad*
	I Went Walking	*Salí de paseo*
	If You Take a Mouse to School	*Si llevas un ratón a escuela*
	This Is the Way We Go to School: A Book About Children Around the World	
	Oh, the Places You'll Go!	
		¡Oh, cúan lejos llegarás!
Transportation / El transporte	*Bear on a Bike*	*Oso en bicicleta*
		El baul de los transportes. Un libro sobre los numeros
	The Journey Home from Grandpa's	
	We All Go Traveling By	
	I Wish I Were a Pilot	
	Transportation— Medios de transporte (Bilingual Book)	
Friends / Los amigos	*A Color of His Own*	*Su propio color*
	Elmer's Friends	*Los amigos de Elmer*
	Margaret and Margarita	*Margarita y Margaret*
	Big Dog...Little Dog	*Perro grande...perro pequeño*
	Should I Share My Ice Cream?	
	We're Different, We're the Same	
	That's What a Friend Is	

GREAT STORYBOOKS

References

Beed, P. L., Hawkins, E. M., and Roller, C. M. (1991). Moving learners toward independence: The power of scaffolded instruction. *The Reading Teacher*, *44*(9), 648-655.Berninger, V. W. (2008). Defining and differentiating dysgraphia, dyslexia, and language learning disability within a working memory model. Brain, behavior, and learning in language and reading disorders, 103-134.

Bruner, J. (1978). The role of dialogue in language acquisition. *The child's conception of language*, *2*(3), 241-256.

California State University. Libros Recomendados en Español/Recommended Books in English about Latinos. *Barahona Center for the study of books in Spanish for Children and Adolescence.* 2007. California State University, San Marcos <http://www.csusm.edu/csb/espanol/>.

Campbell, J. R., Kelly, D. L., Mullis, I. V., and International Association for the Evaluation of Educational Achievement. (2001). *Framework and specifications for PIRLS assessment 2001.* International Study Center.

Campbell, J. R., Kelly, D. L., Mullis, I. V. S., Martin, M. O., & Sainsbury, M. (2001). Progress International Reading Literacy Study (PIRLS). *International Association for the Evaluation of Educational Achievement (IEA), Second Edition. Chestnut Hill, MA, USA: PIRLS International Study Center.*

Carmichael, C., Callingham, R., Watson, J., & Hay, I. (2009). Factors influencing the development of middle school students' interest in statistical literacy. *Statistics Education Research Journal*, *8*(1), 62-81.

Catts, H. W., & Kamhi, A. G. (Eds.). (2005). *The connections between language and reading disabilities.* Psychology Press.

"Children's Defense Fund." *The SAGE Encyclopedia of World Poverty* (n.d.): n. pag.*Children's Defense Fund13.* Children's Defense Fund, 13 Sept. 2016. Web. 12 May 2017.

Coppola, S. (2014). The Images Deficit in the Teaching of Writing. *The Reading Teacher*, *68*(2), 127-127.

Crowe, L. K., Norris, J. A., & Hoffman, P. R. (2000). Facilitating storybook interactions between mothers and their preschoolers with language impairment. *Communication Disorders Quarterly*, *21*(3), 131-146.

DeBaryshe, B. D. (1993). Joint picture-book reading correlates of early oral language skill. *Journal of child language*, *20*(02), 455-461.

Denham, S. A. (1998). *Emotional development in young children.* Guilford Press.

Doyle, B. G., & Bramwell, W. (2006). Promoting emergent literacy and social–emotional learning through dialogic reading. *The Reading Teacher*, *59*(6), 554-564. Elias, M.J. (2003). Academic and social-emotional learning. Educational Practices, 11, 1-31.

Fey, M. E., Catts, H. W., Proctor-Williams, K., Tomblin, J. B., & Zhang, X. (2004). Oral and written story composition skills of children with language impairment. *Journal of Speech, Language, and Hearing Research*, *47*(6), 1301-1318.

Feldman, K., & Denti, L. (2004). High-access instruction: Practical strategies to increase active learning in diverse classrooms. *Focus on Exceptional Children*, *36*(7), 1.

Frost, S. J., Mencl, W. E., Sandak, R., Moore, D. L., Rueckl, J. G., Katz, L., ... & Pugh, K. R. (2005). A functional magnetic resonance imaging study of the tradeoff between semantics and phonology in reading aloud. *Neuroreport*, *16*(6), 621-624.

Gillam, R. B., & Pearson, N. A. (2004). TNL: Test of Narrative Language. *Austin, TX: Pro-Ed.*

Gilliver, M. L., & Byrne, B. (2009). What's in a name? Preschoolers' noun learning performance in relation to their risk for reading disability. *Reading and Writing*, *22*(6), 637-659.

Glenn, C. G., & Stein, N. L. (1980). Syntactic structures and real world themes in stories generated by children. *Urbana: University of Illinois Center for the Study of Reading.*

Gutiérrez-Clellen, V. F. (2002). Narratives in two languages: Assessing performance of bilingual children. *Linguistics and Education*, *13*(2), 175-197.

Hatch, E. (1992). *Discourse and language education.* Cambridge University Press.

Heath, S. B. (1982). What no bedtime story means: Narrative skills at home and school. *Language in society*, *11*(01), 49-76.

Hedberg, N. L., & Westby, C. E. (1993). *Analyzing storytelling skills: Theory to practice.* Communication Skill Builders.

Huennekens, M. E., & Xu, Y. (2010). Effects of a cross-linguistic storybook intervention on the second language development of two preschool English language learners. *Early Childhood Education Journal*, *38*(1), 19-26.

Hudson, J. A., Shapiro, L. R., McCabe, A., & Peterson, C. (1991). From knowing to telling: The development of children's scripts, stories, and personal narratives. *Developing narrative structure*, 89-136.

Jensen, E. (2008). *Brain-based learning: The new paradigm of teaching.* Corwin Press.

Klecan-Aker, J. S., McIngvale, G. K., & Swank, P. R. (1987). Stimulus considerations in narrative analysis of normal third grade children. *Language and speech*, *30*(1), 13-24.

Klecan-Aker, J. S., & Brueggeman, L. (1991). *The expression connection: A structured approach to teaching storytelling to school age children.* Speech Bin.

References

Klecan-Aker, Joan S. & Colson, Karen (2009). Criterion-Referenced Assessment for Language Organization: An Example of Evidence-Based Practice, Forum on Public Policy Online, Spr 2009

Lesaux, N. K., & Siegel, L. S. (2003). The development of reading in children who speak English as a second language. *Developmental psychology*, *39*(6), 1005.

Linan-Thompson, S., Vaughn, S., Prater, K., & Cirino, P. T. (2006). The response to intervention of English language learners at risk for reading problems. *Journal of Learning Disabilities*, *39*(5), 390-398.

Lipka, O., & Siegel, L. S. (2007). The development of reading skills in children with English as a second language. *Scientific Studies of Reading*, *11*(2), 105-131.

Melzi, G. (2000). Cultural variations in the construction of personal narratives: Central American and European American mothers' elicitation styles. *Discourse Processes*, *30*(2), 153-177.

Merritt, D. D., & Liles, B. Z. (1987). Story Grammar Ability in Children with and without Language DisorderStory Generation, Story Retelling, and Story Comprehension. *Journal of Speech, Language, and Hearing Research*, *30*(4), 539-552.

Montgomery, J. W., & Evans, J. L. (2009). Complex sentence comprehension and working memory in children with specific language impairment. *Journal of Speech, Language, and Hearing Research*, *52*(2), 269-288.

Morais, J., Mousty, P., Kolinsky, R., Hulme, C., & Joshi, R. M. (1998). Reading and spelling: development and disorders. *Reading and spelling: development and disorders.*

Ninio, A., & Bruner, J. (1978). The achievement and antecedents of labelling. *Journal of child language*, *5*(01), 1-15.

Noble, K. G., Norman, M. F., & Farah, M. J. (2005). Neurocognitive correlates of socioeconomic status in kindergarten children. *Developmental science*, *8*(1), 74-87.

Parnell, M. M., Amerman, J. D., & Harting, R. D. (1986). Responses of language-disordered children to wh-questions. *Language, Speech, and Hearing Services in Schools*, *17*(2), 95-106.

Poveda, David. "La Ronda in a Spanish Kindergarten Classroom with a Cross-Cultural Comparison to Sharing Time in the USA." *Anthropology & Education Quarterly* 32.3 (2001): 301-325.

Proctor, B. D., Semega, J. L., & Kollar, M. A. (2016). Income and poverty in the United States: 2015. Washington, DC: United States Census Bureau, September.

Rabidoux, P. C., & MacDonald, J. D. (2000). An interactive taxonomy of mothers and children during storybook interactions. *American Journal of Speech-Language Pathology*, *9*(4), 331-344.

Rice, M. L., Bishop, D. V. M., & Leonard, L. B. (2000). Grammatical symptoms of specific language impairment. *Speech and language impairments in children: Causes, characteristics, intervention and outcome*, 17-34.

Raz, I. S., & Bryant, P. (1990). Social background, phonological awareness and children's reading. *British Journal of Developmental Psychology*, 8(3), 209-225.

Shiro, Martha Klein (1998). A discourse analysis approach to evaluate stance in Venezuelan children's narratives. *Dissertation Abstracts International: Section B: the Sciences and Engineering*. *Vol. 58 (8-B)*,

Silliman, E. R., Bahr, R. H., Brea, M. R., Hnath-Chisolm, T., & Mahecha, N. R. (2002). Spanish and English proficiency in the linguistic encoding of mental states in narrative retellings. *Linguistics and Education*, *13*(2), 199-234.

Stein, N. L. (1988). The development of children's storytelling skill. In *Portions of this paper were presented at the Eleventh Annual Boston University Child Language Conference, Oct 17-19, 1986.*. Oxford University Press.

Swanson, L., Fey, M., Mills, C., & Hood, L. (2005). Intervention with children who have specific language impairment. American Journal Of Speech--Language Pathology, 14 (2), 131--143. *Pathology*, *14*(2), 131-143.

Teale, W. H., & Sulzby, E. (1986). *Emergent Literacy: Writing and Reading. Writing Research: Multidisciplinary Inquiries into the Nature of Writing Series*. Ablex Publishing Corporation, 355 Chestnut St., Norwood, NJ 07648.

Tomblin, J. B., Zhang, X., Buckwalter, P., & Catts, H. (2000). The association of reading disability, behavioral disorders, and language impairment among second-grade children. *Journal of child Psychology and Psychiatry*, *41*(4), 473-482.

Treiman, R., Hulme, C., & Joshi, R. M. (1998). Beginning to spell in English. *Reading and spelling: Development and disorders*, 371-393.

Ulatowska, H. K., & Chapman, S. B. (1994). Discourse macrostructure in aphasia. *Discourse analysis and applications: Studies in adult clinical populations*, 29-46.Van Daal, J., Verhoeven, L., & Van Balkom, H. (2007). Behaviour problems in children with language impairment. *Journal of child psychology and psychiatry*, *48*(11), 1139-1147.

Ulatowska, H. K., & Olness, G. S. (2001). Dialectal variants of verbs in narratives of African Americans with aphasia: Some methodological considerations. *Journal of Neurolinguistics*, *14*(2), 93-110.

Vygotsky, L. S. (1980). *Mind in society: The development of higher psychological processes*. Harvard university press.

Wilson, M. S., Fox, B. J., & Pascoe, J. P. (2012). Asking and Answering Questions; Theory & Research Based Intervention.

Weizman, Z. O., & Snow, C. E. (2001). Lexical output as related to children's vocabulary acquisition: Effects of sophisticated exposure and support for meaning. *Developmental psychology*, *37*(2), 265.

References

Westby, C. E., & Simon, C. (1991). Learning to talk, talking to learn: Oral-literate language differences. *Communication skills and classroom success*, 334-357.

Whitehurst, G. J., Adamson, L. B., & Romski, M. A. (1997). Language processes in context: Language learning in children reared in poverty. *Research on communication and language disorders: Contribution to theories of language development*, 233-266.

Zins, J. E. (2001). Examining opportunities and challenges for school-based prevention and promotion: Social and emotional learning as an exemplar. *The Journal of Primary Prevention, 21*(4), 441-446.

Made in the USA
Lexington, KY
14 December 2017